STO

ACPL ITEM
DISCARDED

3 1833 00295 1561

Y0-BUC-197

12-1-69

BIBLIOLOGIA COMICA

or
Humorous Aspects of the Caparisoning and Conservation of Books

By
LAWRENCE S. THOMPSON

ARCHON BOOKS
1068

© 1968, Lawrence S. Thompson

SBN: 208 00712 1
Library of Congress Catalog Card Number: 68-56899
Printed in the United States of America

1517150

To Richard

CONTENTS

ACKNOWLEDGMENTS

The author and publisher gratefully acknowledge the permission to reprint the essays included in this volume.

"Bibliopegia Fantastica" reprinted with permission from the *Bulletin of The New York Public Library*, September, 1944.

"Notes on Bibliokleptomania" reprinted with permission from the *Bulletin of The New York Public Library*, February, 1947.

"A Cursory Survey of Maledictions" reprinted with permission from the *Bulletin of The New York Public Library*, February, 1952.

"Religatum de Pelle Humana" reprinted with permission from *University of Kentucky Libraries Occasional Contributions*, No. 6, 1949.

The reader should bear in mind that these essays were composed during and immediately after World War II and that political conditions of that period are reflected in many comments. Further, certain technological advances such as cheap electrostatic copying have altered many conditions described in these essays.

INTRODUCTION

I rarely read introductions, but admittedly they do help the reviewer seeking instant information. So, let me first draw the triad sacred to critic or student, the triad of purpose, scope and audience. It seems to me that Dr. Lawrence Thompson's purpose is to entertain and to inform, an unbeatable combination. The scope considers the entire library, yet essentially is limited by interest in theft and bookbinding. Finally, the whole will appeal to the bookish minded and anyone fascinated by the foibles of man.

The essays pretty well parallel the author's early career. Fittingly enough, "Notes on Bibliokleptomania" appeared when the 28-year-old former Iowa State College librarian was working for the F.B.I. As a special agent he moved in and out of New York, Washington and Latin America from 1942 to 1945. Along the way he managed to write an essay which celebrates the thief, thereby qualifying himself as suitable subsidiary character in a yet to be written commentary. Some three years later, as head librarian at Western Michigan College of Education, he paid homage to the "lunatic fringe" which collects bindings. Then, in 1949 and 1952, while director of libraries at the University of Kentucky, he elaborated on both the professional thief and bookbinder. Presently he is teaching classical languages at the University of Kentucky and, hopefully, considering some of his later essays for another collection.

Because the time we first met is typical enough of the man, it is worth recounting here briefly. We met when I came to the University of Kentucky as a teacher, and he was director of the library. As I came into his office, he was bent over an ancient upright typewriter rapping away furiously with the single finger by finger tap. The office, as I imagine are all his places of residence for more than a few days, was lined with books and the walls with pictures of respectable and not so respectable book dealers and collectors. When he rose, he looked wonderfully like the stereotype of the slightly rumpled, slightly myopic professor, and while I no longer remember what we said, the impression continued of a genuine scholar. It seemed to me he laughed a great deal, often before the point of the particular story was made. I had the distinct impression of nervous alertness, an impatience with the slowness of speech, and a sensitivity close to downright bashfulness.

Well, this memory somehow helps to explain the shape, style and the charm of the essays collected here. They remind me much of his conversation, the staccato of pictures and sounds, yet never out of order, always supported by a complete command of the subject. What first may appear to be a hit-and-miss approach suddenly turns into an ordered, thoughtful and usually entertaining insight. Here, I think, he differs considerably from the R. L. Garners of this world who go into the jungle hunting for material. Garner sought the apes, and took with him a wire cage. Setting it up, he climbed in and proceeded to wait for the apes. As Edith Sitwell observes: "Unfortunately, the wire cage, chosen for its practical invisibility to imaginative and idealistic minds, always exists during these experiments."

There are no cages here, and the story is particularly fitting for anyone interested in Dr. Thompson's approach. The story is culled from Dame Sitwell's *The English Eccentrics*, a work which I would recommend to anyone who becomes involved in the present collection. Both the late poetess and the present author share a mutual concern with the slightly mad and eccentric aspects of our world. Both share a conviction that to understand ourselves we must appreciate those who choose to walk on the wild side of the street.

Necessarily, the comparison between the gentleman from Kentucky and the Dame from England is only relative. For one thing, while Dame Sitwell was a conjurer, Dr. Thompson is a scholar. His narrative is buttressed with ample footnotes and sources, and a good deal of the charm is his mastery of technical and enumerative matter. In the course of his four essays he draws upon a rich, patiently assembled mass of materials. Two essays in particular reveal his carefully calculated course through obscurity: that on "Notes on Bibliokleptomania," and a more recent piece, "A Cursory Study of Maledictions." The reduction and adaptation of some 200 sources, few of which suggest either laughter or significance, is essentially the triumph of imagination over the recognizably pallid.

In an age which believes that the computer is a short cut to everything, and that the media is more important than the message, a natural criticism of Dr. Thompson's essays is inevitable. What, one may ask, is the point of marshalling all this esoteric paraphernalia? One is inclined to answer in the same key as Louis Armstrong when someone asked him to define jazz. To paraphrase his reply: "If you don't know, baby, there's no good explaining."

Armstrong is right, but for the benefit of those who accept the absurd notion that individuals can be reduced to charts and diagrams, let me at least try an explanation of Dr. Thompson's particular contribution. The author is one of those happy people who believes there is more to life than "they" and "them," who visualizes history in terms of personal names and actions, who is both amused and appalled by the follies of such characters as "let petit Chose." He takes an impious attitude toward history as a movement, and, I believe, toward books and libraries as notations in a systems analysis or computer memory. The extraordinary confrontation of man with any planned organization always seems to end in favor of the man, even in death. In a word, the stuffed figure dressed in his proper professional role of writer, librarian, bookbinder or even thief is given life and movement by Dr. Thompson's incurable interest.

One feels fortunate to have run across the characters who discover human skin as a binding material, manage to steal or prevent the theft of books, or simply suffer from incurable bibliomania. Many are possessed with a morbid, almost pathological notion about books, but invariably they are motivated and influenced by human desires. To have met them is to have encountered life.

So, the essays may be approached at two levels. The first is the obvious, yet to my mind irrelevant level of information and education about books, libraries and collectors. The second, more consequential, is the implied level of reconsidering esoteric, often dull themes in terms of successive personalities and characters; or, as Dame Sitwell might put it, in terms of eccentrics. I think it is to seriously underestimate Dr. Thompson's contribution to evaluate his essays at only the first, and not the second level.

A searching appraisal of the essays may indicate other possible implications, yet this is to run the danger of distorting the obvious. There is a conscious effort here to demonstrate that properly arranged data can be accepted and enjoyed for enjoyment's sake. I'm inclined to let this be quite enough, and leave it to better qualified critics to challenge or cheer this or that statement or citation.

Henry Miller once observed that, "Those who know how to read a man know how to read his books." It would be pompous conceit to say I know either the man or his books that well, but even the most cursory examination of the present collection will support one conclusion about Dr. Thompson—he is a whopping good story teller. This talent is what apparently was alluded to in a brief biographical sketch which noted: "Although of scholarly temperament, Dr. Thompson has a good sense of humor and interest in current problems." While scholarship and humor don't seem mutually exclusive, I'm not quite sure where the "interest in current problems" fits in. As a matter of fact, anyone wishing to forget the present anarchy of today's front page is strongly advised to take up this book. And these days I can think of no greater recommendation.

Bill Katz

BIBLIOLOGIA COMICA

Bibliopegia Fantastica

IN THE WORLD OF BIBLIOMANIA few of the devotees of book arts are more prone to step beyond the lunatic fringe than the collector of bindings. Ever determined to own a "unique" exemplar or almost any binding with colorful associations, the bibliopegic enthusiast will stop at nothing to accomplish his wildest dreams. Quite aside from the sensationalism of the anthropodermic binding, there are book covers which, if gathered into one catalogue, would shed an aura of glamor unknown to bibliophily since the auction at Binche.

It won't be necessary to make a pilgrimage to some distant collection of a bibliopegic crank, for within the walls of The New York Public Library there are many of the more exotic specimens. In the hidden recesses of the Reserve Room there are bindings in strange materials ranging from wallpaper to cork, from tapa cloth to the "skin of a baseball," from fiberglass to a cigar box. A treatise entitled *Shakespeare and Stratford upon Avon* is bound in oak boards from the Holy Trinity Church where Shakespeare was baptised and buried, and Henry Slight's *True Stories of H. M. Ship Royal George* rests on NYPL shelves in the very timbers of that gallant vessel.[1]

But even our own Shakespearian oak cannot claim to be the most ancient wooden binding in this metropolis, for a few blocks downtown there is a 2,000-year-old slab of oak in the possession of Dr. Otto W. Fuhrmann of New York University, put to good use even yet as the cover for a catalogue from Leipzig's Buchgewerbe-Museum.[2] It is a part of a beam once used to support a Roman military bridge at Mainz, identified through the discovery in the same piling of a bronze log

15

stamping tool bearing the number of the Twenty-second Legion, stationed at Mainz soon after Caesar's first crossing of the Rhine. It was discovered about 1880 by H. Klemm.

Personally, I am somewhat more inclined to accept the antiquity of Dr. Fuhrmann's prize than the wood-bound Bibles which homecoming missionaries used to display in the fundamentalist Southern town of my childhood. Vague intimations were made that the wood was hewn from the Mount of Olives not long after the Sermon of Our Lord was delivered; but recent visitors to the Holy Land report that this barren hillside produces no more olives than Calvary produces authentic splinters of the True Cross. Incidentally, returning GIs report that the Cross business still flourishes among the followers of the Prophet. One friend alleges that when in Cairo he was offered a Greek Testament with an inlaid sliver over which were blazoned the words *VERA CRUX.* He declined the purchase, but two weeks later he liberated from a hastily evacuated German air base in Tunisia two identical bindings with the same binder's ticket. Both are resting at present on a mantelpiece in Kalamazoo.

It has apparently been deemed especially appropriate to bind religious books in wood, possibly with the motive of avoiding *cenationum ornamenta* represented by luxury bindings which would detract from their meaning as *studiorum instrumenta.* A recent Duschnes catalogue[3] offered a George V *Book of Common Prayer* (with the Royal Warrant signed by Winston Churchill as Home Secretary) printed on vellum and bound in mahogany boards. Incongruously enough, I once saw this same magnificent Dominican wood used as a cover for a pornographic book peddled on the streets of Ciudad Trujillo. When the seven-century-old Elstow Church was restored in 1880, a few copies of *Pilgrim's Progress* were encased in the remnants of its oak beams. The wooden sides of some choice copies of W. S. Simpson's *St. Paul's Cathedral Library* come from fragments of the beam in the belfry of the great minster which were removed during the restoration of 1893.[4] An American collector, Paul Jourdan-Smith, bound a facsimile of Sir Thomas Browne's *Religio Medici* in thin oak boards which came from the Browne manor in Norwich. NYPL's *Shakespeare and Stratford upon Avon* boasts of a somewhat less fascinating history than an item which was knocked down at Baroness Burdett-Coutts' sale at Sotheby's in 1922. It was a carven cumdach for Shakespeare's plays made of a portion of Herne's Oak and presented to the Baroness by Queen Victoria. The Widow of Windsor had a silver plaque affixed to the inside of the lid reading: "This casket, carved out of Herne's Oak, the tree mentioned in *The Merry Wives of Windsor*, contains the First Quarto edition of Shakespeare's poems, published *anno* 1640, and the still more rare first edition of the dramatic works, published in 1623. The old tree fell down in 1863." The chest and its contents went to America for £8,600.

"Association bindings" of wood, if we may coin the term, are fairly numerous. Especially fascinating is the Burns done up in wooden covers taken from the slats of the bed in which he died.[5] A first edition of *Paradise Lost* brought $17,500 in New York in 1935 due to the fact that it was in brown sheep covering wooden boards fashioned from a rafter originally a part of the house in Westminster where Milton began his masterpiece. Then there was a volume entitled *Aurora Australis*, written, set, printed, and wood-bound in Shackleton's antarctic headquarters. Most of the bindings of this edition consist of beveled boards made from packing cases that had contained provisions, and one English collector has a copy with the word KIDNEYS stamped on the side in capital letters.

Examples of unusual wooden bindings in NYPL's collections afford an abundance of local color. Roy Carlson Colman's collection of poems which he called *The Devil's Playground and the Sea* (La Jolla, California, 1936) is covered with California redwood. Greatorex' *Die Heimat von Oberammergau* is in wooden boards carved about 1900 by a native of that Bavarian hamlet. Considerably less pretentious is the binding of W. A. Penn's *The Soverane Herbe: a History of Tobacco* (New York: Dutton, 1901) put up in cigar-box boards with a title stamped in black on the side.[6] Strictly a bibliophilic *tour de force* is the two-volume edition of Cervantes' *Novelas ejemplares* (Barcelona: Editorial Orbis, 1933) not only bound in cork but actually printed on leaves made from this characteristic product of the Iberian Peninsula.

Wooden bindings are often not merely symbolic but also may prove to be the media for artistic expression. Particularly striking was a creation of George A. Simonds of Washington, D. C., for the National Geographic Society's *Wild Animals of North America*.[7] The cover, a masterpiece of intarsia, represents a moose which is also portrayed in a plate in the book, but no ordinary beast is this:

> The sky is tulip wood from Brazil; the trees, Brazilian rosewood; the moose's body, mottled walnut butt from Australia, and the horns, walnut crotch from the U. S., while the inside of the right horn is African avodoire. The bushes at the front are bubinga from Africa, and the mountains, amaranth from Dutch Guiana, American cherry and walnut. Those water pads are American poplar burl, and the water, American maple crotch. The moose's eye is made of two woods, American white holly and gaboon ebony from Africa. The water seen through the trees is gray harewood from England.

Japanese wood veneer was used as the cover for the February, 1935, issue of *PM; an Intimate Journal for Advertizing Production Managers, Art Directors, and Their Associates*.[8] The Pitman Publishing Company produced a book entitled *Modern Plywood* which was bound in the real McCoy.[9]

Hardly a true library, but nevertheless worthy of mention for the suggestions it might offer to the collector of silvicultural literature, is the so-called "wooden library." Toward the end of the eighteenth century a zoo inspector in Kassel named Schildbach had a collection of native woods set up in the form of books.[10] The spine of each "book" was the rough bark of the tree on which had been pasted red leather labels with the name of the tree in various languages. The polished cross sections of wood served as the side of the "book." One of these sides could be removed, and in the hollow interior there were samples of the leaves, flower, fruit, and seed of the tree as well as a piece of the root. A similar "library" of seventy-nine volumes was known to have been in the possession of the Hungarian National Museum before the Russians occupied the Magyar capital. The Bavarian naturalist Kandid Huler, who died in 1813 in Stellwang near Landshut, was reputed to have owned a "wooden library" consisting of fifty-one "octavo" volumes.

Pitman was hardly an innovator, for many another commercial publisher has brought out bindings sympathetic with the contents of his book. Percy Fitzgerald records that a *Manuel of Woodcarving* was issued by Bemrose and Sons in wooden covers as the publishers' binding.[11] Jacob Riis' *How the Other Half Lives* was originally offered for public sale in what appeared to be the denim from a laborer's overalls.[12] I well remember the beloved poet of my childhood, John Charles McNeill, whose *Lyrics from Cottonland* were bound in gay bandanna not unlike the familiar kerchief my "mammy" wore; and in the earliest stages of the book collecting game a special thrill came with the acquisition of the fictitious biography of one Sandy McNabb, bound in a Royal Stuart tartan and sporting the paradoxically democratic inlay of a Lincoln penny. But neither were so elegant as much more tasteful treasures in NYPL's Reserve Room such as the Limited Editions issue of *Madame Bovary* (1938) in gold silk or the monograph on the Feodoroff Imperial Cathedral in Tzarskoe-Selo which appeared in Moscow in 1915 in brocade with peach silk doublures (not to mention the fact that the local copy is an autographed presentation from Empress Alexandra to Isabel F. Hapgood!).

And of silk and satin there are bindings galore in nearly every collection of any importance. At Samuel Putnam Avery's show at Columbia in 1903 there was a nineteenth-century French almanach entitled *Le perroquet d'amour* suitably

bound for a *belle dame's* boudoir in white satin with the sides
and back hand-painted in colors, cupids in the corners representing the four seasons, and the vintage and a hunting scene
on the side borders.[13] In the same exhibition there was a
similar binding of a *Hommage aux demoiselles*. Mr. Avery's
elegant covers for these dainty bits would hardly be appropriate on the same shelf with NYPL's calico-bound copy of
Shi Beck's *I Ain't A-caring* (Dallas, Texas, 1935) or of *Pele,
the Goddess of Fire* (Hilo, Hawaii, 1907) in its original wrappers of tapa cloth.

It is hardly surprising to observe that tapa cloth is especially
popular with Polynesian binders. Mrs. Hassoldt Davis, wife of
the well-known author of *Islands under the Wind*, was annoyed by the blatant red cover of her husband's first book
and therefore apprenticed herself to a Tahitian "binder" who
mended official records. When she mastered the craft, she
bound many books in tapa cloth. Later on, seeking originality,
she wanted to bind the French government's documents in
Dutch batik, but the master of her shop balked. A special
rarity is Mrs. Davis' limited edition of fifty copies of a humorous poem typed on Chinese wrapping paper, bound in home-
made batik, and inscribed: "This is number —— of an edition
limited to fifty copies, printed upon Chinese parchment, and
bound in batik by Hinny Magoo." And she cherished with
special pride a rat skin tanned with aguacate seed and destined to be the cover of a primary school natural history.[14]

But the real treasure in Polynesian binding is NYPL's copy
of *Te Evanelia na Luka, iritihia ei parau Tahiti* (Moorea,
1818)—the Gospel of St. Luke in plain English—bound in native bark cloth with sides showing a painted fern design in
purple. Another South Sea treasure in NYPL is the first Hawaiian hymnal, compiled by William Ellis and Hiram Bingham
and printed in Oahu in 1828, bound in tortoise shell with a
leather back. Of course, there are numerous copies of *Typee*
and *Omoo* in tapa cloth; and an especial appeal to the exotic
was made in an edition of Don Blanding's poems bound in
Hawaiian hula hula grass.[15]

Mrs. Davis' use of batik has a parallel in the field of commercial publishing, for the novel *Java Girl* was originally invested in Javanese batik, and Mrs. Higginson's *Princess of Java* was issued in similar material. A biography of Mohandas K. Ghandi was bound in *khaddar*,[16] the native homespun of India, and Elbert Hubbard's *Abe Lincoln and Nancy Hanks* was issued by the Roycrofters in a "homespun edition"—a board covered with coarse-meshed burlap, hempen cords for the bands, end sheets of calico paper, and a straw paper jacket.[17] Another odd bit of Lincolniana was *Mary Wife of Lincoln* by Mrs. Kate Helm, grandniece of Mrs. Lincoln, which appeared in 1928 in an edition including many copies having tapestry inserts on the front cover taken from a curtain in the home of Miss Todd (Mrs. Mary Lincoln) in Lexington, Kentucky.[18]

One of the most ironical bindings of modern times adorned Alfred L. Lomax' *Pioneer Woolen Mills in Oregon* issued in 1942 by the Pendleton Woolen Mills of Pendleton, Oregon, and bound by Rudolph Ernst in "twist" woolen suiting. In 1942 most of us would gladly have bought enough of the 300 copies to cut out a wardrobe of somewhat more substantial material than the *Ersatz* trash in which we were shivering. In the nearly mythological days when cotton fabric was plentiful, Elliott White Spring had his *Rise and Fall of Carol Banks* printed on glazed cotton sheets, bound in blue bedspreads from the author's own mills, and jacketed in little hemstitched pillowcases.[19] This monumental tribute to King Cotton is said to be three times heavier than ordinary books printed on paper and bound in boards and linen. Schuster reported a juvenile title bound in material otherwise used for children's clothing.[20]

Among America's most prolific creators of fantasy bindings is Captain Maurice Hamonneau, late of the French Foreign Legion and presently of the bookshop of the American Museum of Natural History. One of the unusual fabrics he has used adorns Clare Boothe Luce's *The Women* in the form of a cloth laminated with gold and silver threads. Within a tiny

opening in the binding he inserted a rattlesnake rattle which
gives an audible warning to the unwary reader who opens the
book.[21] For a handsome binding of documents reproducing
the log of H. M. S. *Bounty* he has used the Union Jack and
bunting signal pennants of the period for end sheets.[22] Captain Hamonneau's cover for his binding of *All Quiet on the
Western Front* is taken from part of a German uniform; but
this is not an altogether novel material, for the Library of
Congress owns a book from the late Czar's library in the
remnants of a shako of a member of the Imperial Guard.

After William Pickering bound the first of his *Diamond
Classics* in purple cloth in 1821, there was a rash of gay and
unusual cloth bindings. Cyril Davenport has reported small,
well-illustrated silk-bound books which were issued commer-
cially in England in the second quarter of the last century.[23]
Unhappily, these books were quite fragile and difficult to repair, and relatively few are still extant in good condition. For
example, in 1825 Jones and Company published a small edition
of *Diamond Poets* in brown silk and somewhat later *The
Lady's Monitor* and *Culled Flowers* (1840), both in red crin-
kled silk. Even in recent times silk has had its attractions for
publishers. Among modern editions aristocratically sporting
silk on NYPL's otherwise democratic shelves is H. L. Findlay's
Book of Scotland, issued in silk plaid by Collins in 1937. And
even at the risk of exposing some unhappy Russian binder
to the NKVD as a bourgeois reactionary, we feel compelled
to mention the local copy of Ivan Kotlyarevski's parody on
the *Aeneid*, issued in blue cloth and embroidered with silken
threads (Kharkov: Derzhavne literaturne vidavnitsvo, 1937).

Literature and history are physically preserved in many
historic cloth bindings. The Newberry Library has a set of
four volumes bound in calico alleged to be from the dresses
of Mrs. Robert Southey,[24] and the British Museum owns a
book similarly encased by Mrs. Wordsworth.[25] Brander Matthews says that Octave Uzanne coveted a copy of the *Légende
des siècles* soberly clad in a fragment of the dark green uniform worn by Hugo at the time of his reception by the

Academy.[26] Knox College in Galesburg, Illinois, owns the famous khaki-bound Bible of General Edmund H. Allenby in its John H. Finley Collection.[27] World War I legend holds that when Allenby was trying to capture Maknessy, he pored over his Bible until he ran across a verse in Samuel I, "And the garrison of the Philistines went out unto the pass of Michmash." Allenby's scouts found the old pass, and the citadel was taken. More British history is preserved in the binding ordered by the Hon. George Napier for the life of the celebrated dwarf, Jeffrey Hudson—a piece of Charles I's silk waistcoat. Another item bound in material from the wardrobe of the same unhappy monarch was knocked down at the Perry sale for £8 8s.[28]

The Holliston Mills' experts hold that starch-filled bookcloth is actually the earliest form of the plastic bindings which have been gaining in popularity in recent years. Their argument is that cornstarch was one of the first plastics,[29] but in modern times there has been a preference for glass plastics. At a cocktail party given on April 7, 1936, by William E. Rudge at 225 Varick Street, there was displayed a volume bound in plexiglas, the colorless, transparent acryllic resin which attained great military importance during World War II.[30] In 1935 Harcourt, Brace published W. C. Pryor's *The Glass Book*, and three years later the National Library Company in West Springfield, Massachusetts, conceived the notion of rebinding a few copies in fiberglass cloth. NYPL owns the rare *Art of Glass*, by Jean Haudicquier de Blancourt (London: Printed for Dan. Brown, 1699) in a binding of colored fiberglass. Brander Matthews reported that Samuel Putnam Avery owned Sauzy's *Marvels of Glass-making* in covers containing glass panels.[31]

These glass bindings for glass books bring us to the most sensational type of fantastic bindings, a branch of the art which we may call sympathetic bibliopegy, or the attempt to make a binding harmonize with the contents of a book. By way of obvious illustrations we might cite examples of *Mein Kampf* in skunk skin executed by Captain Hamonneau and others or the edition of Charles James Fox's *History of the Early Part of the Reign of James the Second* which the bookseller Jeffrye had bound in the skin of Reynard himself.[32] The stories of Baconian enthusiasts who find the works of their favorite author in pigskin are legion.[33] Another wild beast was sacrificed to bibliopegic whim when "Tuberville on Hunting" was bound by Whittaker in deerskin with a silver stag used to decorate the front cover. In general, sympathetic bindings most frequently derive their symbolism from a pun or from the real or legendary characteristics or associations of the animal from which the cover was taken.

The Germans, in particular the late Paul Kersten, excelled in the art of sympathetic binding. Among his masterpieces he has mentioned two works of Darwin and one about him in monkey skin (but none in human skin).[34] A book on hunting emerged from his shop in the skin of a wild hare, and he used dog leather for other volumes of a miscellaneous character. Another rabbit skin covered a collection of pamphlets in the Duke of Roxburghe's library relative to one Mary Tofts of Godalming, Surrey, who had pretended to be confined of rabbits.[35] Horne is able to give the pressmark for the British Museum's copy of Governor Phillips' *Voyage to Botany Bay* (London, 1789) bound in kangaroo skin. And I have seen *Tales of a Wayward Inn* in full Central Park squirrel.

The Limited Editions Club has been particularly assiduous in binding its publications appropriately. Especially striking was an edition of Apuleius in donkey skin, although it was no new idea, inasmuch as Percy Fitzgerald reports having seen the 1501 *Golden Ass* offered by a bookdealer in a similar cover.[36] The Club's *Last of the Mohicans* in fringed buckskin was also attractive, but neither was this an innovation, for some years ago *Hiawatha* appeared in buckskin with Frederic Remington's illustrations.[37] It is further known that all or part of the 1905 edition of *Cache la Poudre: The Romance of a Tenderfoot in the Days of Custer* was bound in fringed buckskin. One of the more unusual bindings of this type is owned by NYPL, W. H. Hudson's *Far Away and Long Ago*, which the Limited Editions Club had bound in Argentine calfskin, part of which had been left in the natural state (without the hair removed).[38] *La Vuelta de Martin Fierro* was once to be had in a similar binding from a street peddler in Guadalajara, but he caught us after a disastrous evening in the local casino. In the same humor Captain Hamonneau bound a book on big game hunting in Africa in lion skin with the fur intact.[39]

Other examples of un-dehaired leather used with good effect have come from Mr. H. W. Tribolet of the Extra-Binding Department of R. R. Donnelley and Sons. One of his prizes was a zebra hide for Kipling's *Jungle Book*, with a very interesting effect obtained by using the spine of the beast down the backbone of the book.[40] Still another exotic hide which came out of Mr. Tribolet's shop with the hair in pristine condition was a gnu-skin covering for an album. Instead of working with a whole hide, the binders made up the cover from many small fragments about two or three inches in size and of irregular shapes inasmuch as the client could not supply the rare skin in any other form. The pieces were taken to a furrier who skillfully sewed them together to form a larger skin.

Few beasts of the field do not enjoy some intellectual distinction by having had relatives whose mortal remains were curled up around good books. When the importation of leather hides from Europe was stopped at the beginning of World War II, Tribolet and his colleagues were forced to ingenious devices with leathers of various provenance. Experiments with buffalo hide were especially rewarding in the case of larger books. It is said to bear a close resemblance to morocco goatskin, although it is more economical since the skins are considerably larger than goat. Animals such as horses, Bengal tigers,[41] kangaroos,[42] hippopotami, and antelopes, who ordinarily have rather slight academic pretensions, have departed from Captain Hamonneau's bench astride learned tomes. Paul Kersten knew of seals,[43] dogs, apes, cats, and elephants who wound up in a library instead of in a veterinary museum.[44]

In the 1870's the columns of the *Intermédiaire des chercheurs et curieux* were haunted by persistent reports of eccentric bindings in the library of one Lucien de Rosny, whose sale took place on May 15, 1874. Included in his collection were skins of cats, marmot (colored and buff), crocodile, mole, royal tiger, Canadian black wolf, otter, rattlesnake, polar bear, and seal.[45] Sealskin is by no means a stranger in the bindery, although Charles Roux has commented: ". . . ne se fait guère que dans certaines tanneries anglaises; très solide, le grain rappelle en plus petit celui des peaux de truie."[46] Unquestionably seal is a fine leather, and there is little doubt but that it is a rare curiosity among binding leathers today only because of international conventions regulating seal hunting.

Even the hides of birds of the air have not been safe from the bibliopegist seeking a new thrill. Schuster speaks of bindings in ostrich and swan skin, and Barton's essay on Captain Hamonneau is illustrated with a photograph of Rosenthal and Harting's *Ostriches and Ostrich Farming* bound in the skin of that flightless fowl.[47] But perhaps the most astounding statement of the provenance of a book's cover is found in the annotation on the catalogue card for NYPL's copy of Thomas William Lawson's *The Krank: His Language and What It Means* (on baseball): "In original covers, made of the 'skin of a baseball.' "

Whether the celebrated breeches of Mordaunt Cracherode, the father of one of the British Museum's greatest benefactors, were actually buckskin, I know not; but it is certain that few trousers ever boasted a more exotic history or ended up in a more appropriate place. The tale begins with the reverent account made by Frognall Dibdin to explain the financial basis for the Cracherodian collection:

> Mordaunt Cracherode, the father of the Rev. C. M. Cracherode, of celebrated BOOK-FAME, went out to make his fortune, as commander of the Marines, in Anson's ship. He returned, in consequence of his share of the prize money, a wealthy man. Hence the property of his son and hence the *Biblioteca Cracherodiana, in the British Museum.*[48]

But Dibdin, incorrigible gossip, could not stop here with his tale of the old marine colonel, and he goes on to propagate the droll legend that the elder Cracherode returned from the Ansonian odyssey clad "in the identical buckskins which he wore on leaving England" (and, furthermore, that they had been the objects of his "exclusive attachment" during the entire voyage!). And, lending a final aura of bibliophile romance to these "circumnavigating unmentionables," Dibdin broadly suggests that one particular volume in the Cracherode collection is bound in a piece from these selfsame trousers![49]

The collector could hardly contemplate this Cracherodian rarity without longing for other marine bindings such as *Moby Dick* in the skin of an albino whale or *Casuals of the Sea* in a strip of denim from a stoker's overalls. If any of Captain Hamonneau's bindings in canvas sail[50] ever come under the hammer, they will undoubtedly fetch handsome prices. While the tragic history of Dr. Mudd of Shark Island fame has never been, to my knowledge, bound in the skin of those fearsome denizens of the moat of his fortress prison, there is an abundance of examples of books in sharkskin. According to Mr. Tribolet, it was a very difficult leather to handle on the occasion when he used it for binding in the early thirties. Hugo F. Wagner, noted binder of the former city of Breslau, had the same experience with sharkskin, reporting that the grain was so coarse that it was satisfactory only as an inlay or in work where hinges and additional decoration are unnecessary.[51] He made a stationery portfolio in sharkskin with the center third covered by snakeskin laced to the shark; and he committed an unconscious act of sympathetic bibliopegy when he bound an album in sharkskin with a colored inlay of a coat of arms—a gift for a Nazi cabinet minister! In a gentler age when German binders boasted of a different tradition, Paul Kersten bound Pierre Loti's *Fisherman of Iceland* in sharkskin.[52]

The Avery show at Columbia in 1903 was noteworthy for its ichthyological style.[53] The Grolier Club's Izaak Walton exhibition catalogue of 1893 was bound for Mr. Avery by

Tiffany in covers of Javanese shark with borders of Florida gar pike. The seal of the Club and the famous anagram ΙΧθγΣ both in silver, were fastened to the cover. The linings of dark green watered silk were tooled in gold to show a swimming fish. The carved fish on the ribbon bookmark finished off this bibliopegic aquarium.

Ichthyological bibliopegy is a relatively new discovery in the history of the ancient craft of binding. While the Ambrosian Library in Milan is alleged to own a medieval document on fish parchment with letters in golden characters,[54] the earliest reference on record to a binding in fishskin is in a manual to which Paul Kersten refers as Zeidlers Buchbinder-Philosophie (Hall near Magdeburg, 1708). Kersten quotes from Zeidler a discussion of horn books in which it is stated that:

> Such horn book covers may be made for smaller books from eelskin, but larger books may also be bound in it if only it extends over the spine. And an eelskin needs no preparation except that it be well stretched when the body is flayed. It excels all parchments in firmness, and books bound therein seem to be in nothing less than a harness. I believe that similar larger hides of ocean fishes could be secured and used for bindings of books to great use, a matter of which little has been known heretofore.[55]

While there are very few recent examples of books bound in eelskin, there is an abundance of tomes in hides of other types of marine fauna.

In modern times serious consideration has been given to fishskin tannage in Germany during both wars. In that unhappy land leather was so scarce during World War I as to prompt rumors that the Boche tanned the skin of his fellow men, and during the Nuremberg trials evidence was actually introduced and admitted to prove that the beasts of Belsen and Buchenwald had become expert in this macabre art. On the whole, however, more attention was given to tannage of integuments of fishes than of humans. For example, the tannery of Hermann G. Schmid in Neumünster, Holstein, actually tried fishskin tannage on a large scale during World War II. Captain C. F. Payen of the British Intelligence Objectives Sub-Committee has given a detailed account of the tannage which may be employed by any binder who receives an order for a sympathetic cover for *The Compleat Angler*.[56]

Pioneering work in this field had been done by one Franz Martini when he was stationed at Solos-on-the-Sambre (Belgium) with his regiment in August, 1916.[57] One day while on K. P. duty he observed how the clippfish was skillfully flayed by the cooks before frying and the skins discarded. His innate Prussian sense of thrift and his previous experience as a binder for Lüderitz and Bauer in Berlin inspired him to attempt a new type of parchment binding made of clippfish skin. He bound several Wehrmacht documents with such success that he was encouraged to continue his experiments.

Martini reported that fishskin parchment was actually superior to the customary product made from sheep and calfskin in respect both to strength and to flexibility, and he was even able to bind larger books by sewing two or more of the skins together. The parchment was tested by the Reichsprüfungsanstalt in Lichterfeld and found to be of highest quality. One of its most attractive characteristics was its transparency, and Martini was able to achieve notable results by placing various types of marbled papers beneath the skin. Even such a high authority as Bogeng saw real commercial possibilities in clippfish skin,[58] even though he viewed other types of fish and reptile skins as mere curiosities.

Throughout the twenties and thirties few binding shows failed to display fishskin bindings rudely snatched from the depths of the seven seas. Of course, no Strindberg has yet turned up in *luttefisk*, and *Abie's Irish Rose* in *gefüllte Fisch* is as yet unreported; but there have been copies of *Tom Sawyer* in river cat and a whole shelf of rare Schoolcraft titles in lake trout from the chill waters of Mackinac. Some efforts have been made to commercialize fishskin tannage, and one Edward Goerk of New York even secured U. S. Patent no. 3,310,581 (issued August 14, 1937; published August 6, 1940) to process of fishskin tannage.[59] However, there is no evidence that any United States tanner has ever been quite so enterprising as Hermann G. Schmid along these lines.

Perhaps the chief reason for the failure of fish leather to attain popularity is the relative expense of processing it. Then too, as Mrs. A. L. Benedict, an extra-binder of Buffalo, put it, "People do not seem enthusiastic over those queer materials, and their colors do not make effective exhibition books."[60] Her sharkskin (reported by her as "more durable than morocco, but more expensive") and codskin bindings were rejected by the jury of a Columbia University exhibition, but at the same time two of her morocco bindings with gold tooling were accepted by the Grand Salon des Artistes Français.

Closely related to fishskin bindings are book covers in the skins of various reptiles.[61] In many instances such bindings attain rare heights of bibliopegic wit, often as not reptilian in tone. Thus Uzanne reports a Marquis de Sade in boa constrictor as symbolic of the moral venom of that gentleman's literary productions.[62] And surely there was some symbolism, however, unrelated to the de Sade case, in the binding of the Deutsche Bücherei copy of Max Dauthendey's *Des grossen Krieges Not*, published during World War I by the Deutscher Verein Medan at Deli on the east coast of Sumatra. Dauthendey was interned at the time the volume was published, and he directed that it be firmly encased in the hide of local boa.

Unhappily, no competent binder was present to immortalize a venomous castigation of publishers by the late Thomas Wolfe some ten or twelve years ago. It was a cold December night closer to dawn than to midnight when the great novelist was banging away at his ancient typewrier in the old Chelsea Hotel, vainly trying to curb the rich flow of his poetic inspiration to a mere thousand pages. Suddenly he leapt from his stool, stomped across a floor littered with peanut hulls and crumpled manuscript, leveled an accusing finger at a rattlesnake skin, a gift of Marjorie Rawlings, and shouted, "The portrait of a publisher!"

Snakeskin bindings are no jobs for amateurs. Mrs. Benedict,

who had considerable experience with serpentine bibliopegy, reported that she had purchased numerous snakeskins in Paris but that they were not sturdy enough for full bindings and should be used rather as inlays.[63] On the other hand, highly successful work in watersnake leather was executed by students of the Höhere Graphische Fachschule in Berlin.[64] Captain Hamonneau met with success in preventing too rapid drying of snakeskins by stuffing damp paper under the skin as it was stretched out over the boards; and one of his proudest creations was a python skin cover on a work by the late Dr. Raymond L. Ditmars.

Alligator and crocodile hides not monopolized by manufacturers of ladies' shoes and pocketbooks have not infrequently found their way to library shelves. Unhappily, it is the duty of a thorough investigator to report at least one glaring violation of the basic principles of sympathetic bibliopegy at this point. The monstrosity in question was an edition of Emerson in alligator hide unearthed by Brander Matthews in one of his rambles through antiquarian bookshops (probably in the selfsame one that offered a *Book of Common Prayer* in snakeskin). The diplomatic chronicler of old and new bookbindings tried gallantly to rectify this display of bad taste by suggesting that the saurian integument would be more appropriate for Théophile Gautier's *Une nuit de Cléopâtre* with its crocodilian reminiscences of the Nile, while the ophidian hide would have been far better suited to Captain Bourke's *Snake-Dance of the Moquis of Arizona*. Paul Kersten bound Gerstäcker's *Unter dem Äquator* in the hide of a young alligator and argued on the basis of this experience that only the belly side of this beast was suitable for book covers.[65] This is undoubtedly true in the case of older reptiles of this branch of the family, but I once saw an entire edition of a history of the Isthmus of Tehuantepec bound in young alligators with the head still attached to the skin.

Lizards as well as alligators have become dragons of the book world. Captain Hamonneau has used komodo dragon skin with success.[66] Paul Kersten frequently came by skins of the oriental giant lizard in many colors, gray, yellowish, or greenish, and usually highly polished for the trade. In one such skin he bound a tale of a Parisian model, the German title of which was *Die Eidechse*. During a brief stay in Santiago de Cuba during the last war I was shown a manuscript *Historia del Doctor Goebbels* which an Antillian patriot had bound in a number of chameleon skins pieced together rather crudely; and an unauthenticated political legend holds that during the height of the "Hate-Roosevelt" era a political club which will remain anonymous had the late president's campaign speeches bound in the same material.

Amphibians as well as true reptiles have been subjected to the whim of bibliophiles. An uncautioned note culled from the *Mémorial de la librairie française*[67] states that bookbinders in India had met with success in using frogskins. With the aid of certain dyes it is possible to lend these hides the most delicate colors, and the leather is extremely soft. Kersten's hemispheric search for exotic materials also brought the Indian frog to his studio. Apparently his specimen had not been dyed, for he describes the hide as yellowish-brown, with dark brown spots. He was able to use the larger skins for duodecimos, but the smaller ones were barely large enough for the spine of a book of this format.[68] August Wagner and Johannes Paessler report that the East Asiatic water frog *(Rana nigramaculata)* of Japan is just as adaptible for pocket wares as snakeskin and sometimes comes in pelts as long as 13 cm.[69]

Of other amphibians the tortoise has also contributed to the world of books, although if anyone has used his hide, it must have been for a separate print of the monumental treatise of Phelax von und zu Narreneck und Witzenwinkel, *Laut- und Formenlehre der Giraffensprache, eine Einführung.*[70] On the other hand, there are well authenticated examples of tortoiseshell bindings. Bric-a-brac shops all over the Caribbean are full of albums and address books with covers of tortoise shell, and in past centuries the most accomplished artists have seen its possibilities. In 1936 Sotheby offered *A Week's Preparation for the Sacrament* in a tortoise-shell binding with the following note:

> It is probable that all these bindings were made in France about the middle of the 17th century and that some of them, not used at the time, were exported later to England and used for suitable volumes of a convenient size: the book is only attached to the binding by a cord at the head and foot of the spine.[71]

The other bindings referred to were once in Lady Wolseley's collection, sold by Sotheby on October 18, 1918, as lot 265, and two in Mme. Whitney Hoff's library (nos. 188 and 276). At least two tortoise-shell bindings other than NYPL's Hawaiian hymnal are known to exist in the United States (Newberry Library).

While we can hardly regard jeweled bindings, once the order of the day for powerful and wealthy monarchs, as curiosities, there are certain oddities in this general field. Blumenthal knew of a life of Jim Brady whose cover was adorned with a diamond chip.[72] In the same vein he tells of a Rockefeller biography with a dime embedded in the cover, but even this baronial gesture was little beside the luxurious "silver library" of Duke Albrecht of Prussia.[73] Many of the great collections of rare books in America boast of choice bindings in silver, often the highest expressions of the art of the smith. It is still possible to place orders for silver book covers with a few *platerías* in Guadalajara.

While jeweled bindings belong to the past, it is not unknown even today for binders to use semi-precious and artistically wrought materials. Such was the case with a notable binding mentioned by Brander Matthews, a copy of Théodore Deck's *La faience* decorated with panels of pottery, one of which was a portrait of the author executed at his own ceramic works. It would seem altogether probable that this unusual and imaginative work is identical with the binding attributed to Charles Meunier in the catalogue of the Walters sale.[74] A similar type of binding was once observed in the shop of a Copenhagen antiquarian dealer, an account of the Royal Porcelain Factory with panels in its own characteristic sky blue product. A considerably more exotic but none the less handsome binding was executed by Captain Hamonneau in jade.

The rich imagination of modern binders has rejected few materials as unsuitable for book covers. Sigmund Spaeth's *Barber Shop Ballads*, with an introduction by Lardner, has phonograph records in the back and front pockets.[75] One of the most romantic tales about D'Annunzio's reading habits holds that he had part of his library bound in rubber so that he could read in the bathtub without being apprehensive lest water damage the covers. Somewhat more serious attempts have been made to use rubber for bindings. A British patent, number 424,774, was granted to one A. A. Fortier of Paris for binding books and ledgers in rubber.[76]

Some of the most fantastic bindings have been created with the commonest material of the bookbinder, paper. Essad Bey reports books bound in counterfeit banknotes, confiscated pornographic iconography, and inflation currency. A financier showed him a copy of his privately printed memoirs bound in shares of his bankrupt enterprises.[77] We all know the tale of how *The Vicksburg Citizen*, which its editors gallantly sent to press during the siege of 1863, came off in wall paper, the only substance in that beleagured city suitable for receiving typographic impressions. Genial Randolph G. Adams of the William L. Clements Library came out with a bulletin of "Thanks to Michigan Alumni from the Clements Library"[78] printed on wall paper with the patriotic motive of relieving pressure from already strained civilian allotments of paper for 1944. But NYPL owns far greater rarities actually bound in this versatile product. Cotton Mather's *An Epistle to the Christian Indians* (Boston, 1706) is bound in wrappers of contemporary wall paper which is pasted to the first and last leaves. Another early American wall paper is preserved in NYPL's copy of a booklet captioned *Circulating Library and For Sale* issued in 1806 by bookseller Charles Pierce of Portsmouth, New Hampshire. Charles Henry Bertie's *Story of the Royal Hotel and the Theatre Royal, Sydney* (Sydney, 1927), also in NYPL, preserves some of the romance of this hostelry in its covers, once a portion of the dining room wall papers. But the longest and most fascinating story of unusual bookbinding materials is not that of an everyday product such as paper, but rather the rarest of all products of the tannery, human skin. The integument of *homo sapiens* was used time and again during the eighteenth and nineteenth centuries for covering books, often titles with macabre contents to match the covers. Many American libraries own examples of anthropodermic bindings, for example, the Boston Athenaeum, the Newberry, Stanford University's Lane Medical Library, to mention only three in each major sector of this great humane nation. To date, however, no such binding has turned up in NYPL's collections, and until it does, there will be no need to enlighten our readers further concerning this branch of bibliopegic science.[79]

1517150

Notes . . .

1. For a detailed account of this publication see Walter Hart Blumenthal, "A Blockhead's Bookshelf," *Reading and Collecting*, II (no. 3 Feb./March, 1938), 18.

2. "Curiosa," *Bookbinding Magazine*, XXI (no. 5, May, 1935), 36.

3. Philip C. Duschnes, *Seventy-five Choice Books* (New York, 1946; Catalogue no. 75), 5.

4. Blumenthal, *op. cit.*, 20.

5. *ibid.*, p. 18.

6. See also Hermann Schuster, "Kostbare und seltene Einbandstoffe in der Deutschen Bücherei," *Archiv für Buchgewerbe und Gebrauchsgraphik*, LXXII (1935), 296.

7. Description and illustration in "Bindery Brevities," *Bookbinding and Book Production*, XXV (no. 2, Feb., 1937), 34. See also article on Simonds in "Bindery Brevities," *Bookbinding and Book*

Production, XXIV (no. 2, Aug., 1936), 36. Another interesting example of intarsia by binder Reese C. David is reported in "Novel Extra Binding Method Uses Covers Inlaid with Natural Woods," *Bookbinding and Book Production,* XXIV (no. 6, Dec., 1936), 38.

8. Accompanying article by Harrison Elliott, "Japanese Wood Veneer," PM, I (no. 6, Feb., 1935), 24.

9. "1 for the Book," *Bookbinding and Book Production,* XXXVI (no. 1, July, 1942), 27.

10. H. D. I., "Holzbibliotheken," *Die Bücherstube,* II (1923/1924), 64.

11. *The Book Fancier, or the Romance of Book Collecting* (New York: Scribner and Medford, 1886), p. 121.

12. Brander Matthews, *Bookbindings, Old and New* (London: George Bell, 1896), p. 154.

13. *Catalogue raisonée; Works on Bookbinding, Practical and Historical; Examples of Bookbinding of the XVIth to XIXth Centuries, from the Collection of Samuel Putnam Avery, A. M., Exhibited at Columbia University Library MDCCCCIII* (New York: Privately printed, 1903), p. 70. It is interesting to note that in the Middle Ages precious fabrics served as book jackets (*camisae* or *mantergiae*) to protect even more valuable book covers. See Bibliophile Jacob (Paul Lacroix), *Curiosités de l'histoire des Arts* (Paris: Alphonse Delahaye, 1858), p. 168.

14. Hassoldt Davis, "Bookbinding in the South Seas," *Scribner's Magazine,* XCIX (1936), 120–121.

15. Blumenthal, "Case Histories," *Bookbinding and Book Production,* XXX (no. 6, Dec., 1939), 17.

16. Blumenthal, "Case Histories," *Bookbinding and Book Production,* XXX (no. 4, Oct., 1939), 18–19.

17. Picture and description in advertisement in *The Roycrofter,* VI (no. 4, Feb., 1932), iv.

18. Blumenthal, "Case Histories," *Bookbinding and Book Production,* XXX (no. 5, Nov., 1939), 16.

19. "Well Dressed Book," *Bookbinding and Book Production,* XIV (no. 6, Dec., 1931), 46–47, with picture.

20. *op. cit.,* p. 296.

21. Florence von Wien, "Bookbinder: a 60-second Closeup," *This Week Magazine,* July 22, 1945, p. 2 (magazine section of *New York Journal American*).

22. Vernon Pope, "No. 1 Cover Man," *Redbook,* LXXXIV (Nov., 1944), 35 (with a photograph of Captain Hamonneau and some of his bindings).

23. *Byways among English Books* (New York: Frederick A. Stokes, 1927), p. 74–75.

24. See Walter Salt Brassington, *A History of the Art of Bookbinding with Some Account of the Books of the Ancients* (New York: Macmillan, 1894), 252, for further comment on bindings in dresses of literary ladies.

25. Holbrook Jackson, *The Anatomy of Bibliomania* (London: Soncino Press, 1930; two volumes), II, 79.

26. *op. cit.*, p. 156–157.

27. "Historic Bible at Knox," *Michigan State College Friends of the Library News*, III (nos. 1 and 2, winter/spring, 1946), 4.

28. Fitzgerald, *op. cit.*, p. 121–122.

29. Advertisement of the Holliston Mills, Norwood, Massachusetts, in *Publishers' Weekly*, CXLIX (Feb. 2, 1946), 891.

30. "Bindery Brevities," *Bookbinding and Book Production*, XXV (no. 5, May, 1937), 38, 40.

31. *op. cit.*, p. 154.

32. Herbert P. Horne, *The Binding of Books* (London: Kegan Paul, Trench, Trübner, 1894; *Books about Books*), p. 41; Brassington, *op. cit.*, p. 251; and Charles Blanc, *Grammaire des arts décoratifs* (Paris: Librairie Renouard, 1882), 434.

33. E. g., Gustav Erich Adolf Bogeng, *Der Bucheinband: ein Handbuch für Buchbinder und Bücherfreunde* (Halle a. d. S.: Wilhelm Knapp, 1940; second edition), §76.

34. "Kurioses Einbandmaterial," *Die Heftlade*, I (1922/1924), 11.

35. Fitzgerald, *op. cit.*, p. 121.

36. *ibid.* The *Catalogue raisonée* of the Avery show at Columbia lists an interleaved notebook with leaves from the skin of an ass, bound in embroidered canvas from the time of Charles I (p. 69).

37. Blumenthal, "Case Histories," *Bookbinding and Book Production*, XXX (no. 6, Dec., 1939), 17.

38. The curious line of Alfred de Musset, "Le scandale est de mode, il se relie en veau," suggests the possibility of sensational effects in the use of this otherwise commonplace skin. See Louis Octave Uzanne, *Dictionnaire bibliosophique* (Paris: Imprimé pour les Sociétaires de l'Académie des beaux livres, bibliophiles contemporain en l'an de grâce bibliomanique, 1896), p. 358, and L. Derome, *La reliure de luxe* (Paris: E. Rouveyre, 1888), p. 20.

39. Donald Richmond Barton, "The Book and the Beast," *Natural History*, XLIV (1939), 119.

40. An illustration of a book by Captain Hamonneau in undehaired zebra hide may be seen in "Bookbinder Uses Strange Materials," *Popular Science Monthly*, CXXXVI (May, 1940), 89.

41. Adorns Champion's *With the Camera in Tigerland*, according to Pope, *op. cit.*

42. Cyril James Humphries, *The Book, Its History and Development* (New York: Peter Smith, 1931), tells of a book in the British Museum lettered "kangaroo" on the outside.
43. There is a picture of one of Kersten's sealskin bindings in Bogeng's "Neue Einbände von Paul Kersten," *Archiv für Buchbinderei*, XVII (1917), 14–16.
44. "Die in der Buchbinderei verwendeten Materialien," *Archiv für Buchbinderei*, XXVII (1927), 132. For another catalogue of exotic skins used in binding, see "Reliure en peau humaine," *La bibliophila*, IV (1902/1903), 332.
45. e. g., Un vieil abonné, "Reliures singulières," *Intermédiaire des chercheurs et curieux*, XVI (1883), 747–748, and Paul Pinson, "Reliures excentriques," *Intermédiaire des chercheurs et curieux*, XLII (1900), 917–918.
46. *Pour le relieur, amateur ou professionnel; procédés, formules, recettes, tours de mainset "trucs" de toutes sortes pour le brochage, la reliure, la marbroure, la réparation des livres* (Paris: Dunod, 1926), p. 44. Horne, *op. cit.*, p. 40, refers vaguely to "the books of Iceland covered in seal-skin."
47. "Freaks," *Bookbinding Magazine*, XXII (no. 3, Sept., 1935), 34, reports a book bound in ostrich *feathers!*
48. *The Library Companion; or, The Young Man's Guide and the Old Man's Comfort, in the Choice of a Library* (London: Printed for Harding, Triphook, and Lephart, 1824; the "Breeches" edition), p. 384.
49. See also Brassington, *op. cit.*, p. 251–252, and Archer Taylor, "Books Made of Unusual Materials," *American Notes and Queries*, V (1945), 29.
50. Executed during the period prior to World War I when he was serving in the French merchant marine; see Barton, *op. cit.*, p. 120.
51. "Zeitgemässe Einbandkunst—neue Werkstoffe," *Archiv für Buchbinderei*, XXXVIII (1938), 54–56.
52. "Kurioses Einbandmaterial," *loc. cit.*, p. 11.
53. *Catalogue raisonée*, p. 104–105.
54. Bogeng, "Fischleder und Fischpergament," *Zeitschrift für Bücherfreunde*, n. s., IX (1917, Beiblatt), 313. Some additional references on this matter would seem to be appropriate in a postbellum age of leather shortages: "Bücher in Fischhaut-Einband," *Buchdrucker*, XII, (1935), 64–66; Ernst Collin, "Bucheinbände aus Fischhäuten," *Graphische Jugend*, II (1934), 247–249; "Reliures en peaux de poissons," *La reliure*, XLV (1935), 13–14; "Rybí kuze jako knihvazacsky materiál," *Typografia*, XLII (1935), 89; H. W. Stein, "Was will der Fisch beim Buchbinder?" *Welt und*

Wissen, XXIII (1934), 266–268; and F. Weisse, "Fischhaut–Fischleder–Fischpergament," *Das deutsche Buchbinderhandwerk*, L (1935), 310.

55. "Kurioses Einbandmaterial," *loc. cit.*, p. 10.

56. *Some Aspects of the German Leather Industry* (London: H. M. Stationery Office, [1945?]; British Intelligence Objectives Sub-Committee, *Final Report*, no. 50, *Item* no. 22), p. 37.

57. Detailed accounts of Martini's experiments may be found in his article "Fischhaut zu Bucheinbänden," *Archiv für Buchgewerbe*, LVI (1919), 19–21; F. Marle, "Reliures en peaux de poissons," *Papyrus*, XV (1934), 588; Bogeng, "Betrachtungen und Mitteilungen," *Archiv für Buchbinderei*, XVII (1917), 10–11; and Kersten, "Klippfischhaut," *Archiv für Buchbinderei*, XVII (1917), 23.

58. "Betrachtungen und Mitteilungen," *loc. cit.*, p. 11.

59. See "Cuirs de poisson transparents et minces, teints," *Le cuir technique*, XXX (1941), 270.

60. Letter to the editor of *Bookbinding and Book Production*, XXIII (no. 3, March, 1936), 44.

61. A general note was published by R. Pflüger, "Reptilienleder in der Buchbinderei," *Allgemeiner Anzeiger für Buchbindereien*, L (1935), 310.

62. *Caprices d'un bibliophile* (Paris: Rouveyre, 1878), p. 114.

63. "Bindery Brevities," *Bookbinding and Book Production*, XXIII (no. 5, May, 1936), 38.

64. Illustrations in *Archiv für Büchbinderei*, XXXIV (1934), facing p. 71.

65. "Kurioses Einbandmaterial," *loc. cit.*, p. 9.

66. "Bookbinder uses Strange Materials," *loc. cit.*

67. X (1903), 208; see also Albert Cim[okowski], *Le livre: historique-fabrication-achat-classement-usage et entretien* (Paris: Ernst Flammarion, 1905–1908; five volumes), III, 293, note 1.

68. "Kurioses Einbandmaterial," *loc. cit.*, p. 12.

69. *Handbuch für die gesamte Gerberei und Lederindustrie* (Leipzig: Deutscher Verlag, 1925; two volumes), I, 453.

70. *In* Simplicius von Teufeldreck, ed., *Noch nie beschriebene Wunder der Tierwelt* (Schlaraffenstadt i. P.: Münchhausen und Schwarzekunst, 1799; six volumes), III, iv, 1065–2342.

71. *Catalogue of Valuable Printed Books . . . Comprising . . . Tortoise Shell and Other Decorative Bindings . . . Which Will Be Sold by Auction . . . on 27th of July, 1936* (London: Sotheby, 1936), p. 40.

72. "Case Histories," *Bookbinding and Book Production*, XXX (no. 6, Dec., 1939), p. 17.

73. Paul Schwenke and K. Lange, *Die Silberbibliothek Herzog Albrechts von Preussen und seiner Gemahlin Anna Maria* (Leipzig: Hiersemann, 1894), and T. A. Fischer, "The Silver Library of Duke Albrecht of Prussia," *The Collector*, IX (1905), 157–164.

74. *Four centuries of French Literature, Mainly in Superb Bindings* (New York: Parke-Bernet Galleries, 1941).

75. Blumenthal, "Case Histories," *Bookbinding and Book Production*, XXX (no. 3, Sept., 1939), p. 25.

76. "Patent for Rubber Bindings Granted to Paris Inventor," *Bookbinding and Book Production*, XXII (no. 3, Sept., 1935), 44.

77. "Der Einband aus Menschenhaut," *Die literarische Welt*, IV (no. 31, Aug. 3, 1928).

78. *Bulletin of the William L. Clements Library*, XLII (1944).

79. Elsewhere I have gone into the mysteries of this gruesome topic. See my studies, "Promptuary of Anthropodermic Bibliopegy," *The Book Collectors' Packet*, IV (no. 2, Oct., 1945). 15–17; "The Folklore of Tanned Human Skin," *Hide and Leather and Shoes*, CXI (January 12, 1946), 20, 23, 34, 36; and "Tanned Human Skin" (from the medical viewpoint), *Bulletin of the Medical Library Association*, XXXIV (1946), 93–102. Lively discussions may also be found in the columns of *American Notes and Queries*, *Notes and Queries*, and the *Intermédiaire des chercheurs et curieux*.

Notes on Bibliokleptomania

"SI L'ON VEUT me séduire, on n'a que m'offrir des livres."[1] Seguier probably coined this aphorism in an egotistical mood, but the temptation has been an almost universal one. There are few bookmen who have not succumbed, at least in a minor sort of way, notably in the matter of delinquency in returning borrowed books. When some patient legal scholar compiles the Pitaval of biblioklepts, the roll call will look more like a learned congress than a police show-up.

In spite of the great interest always shown in individual sensational thefts, only two authorities have paid any serious attention to the problem of the biblioklept as a larger phenomenon. However, both Albert Cim's *Amateurs et voleurs de livres*[2] and Gustav Bogeng's essay. "Buch und Verbrechen" in his *Streifzüge eines Bücherfreundes*[3] are essentially pleasant *causeries* rather than attempts to give a broad survey of the problem as a whole and to touch upon all of its implications. Still, what Bogeng calls a "Pitaval of bibliokleptomania" would be a worthy task. Possibly when bibliothecal caution has compelled us to observe the last rites of sepulchre on the open-shelf system, somebody may have time to compile a register of all hitherto recorded thefts from public libraries; but no matter what precautions may be taken, as long as there are collections, public and private, and collectors—*et amici*—biblioklepts of some sort will be with us.

Just as no attempt is made in the present study to record any but the most important cases, so also must there be a definite limitation on the amount of space devoted to certain aspects of bibliokleptomania. The psychological, legal, and sociological implications alone would provide ample material for ten years' worth of dissertations in some of our library schools. Viktor Gardthausen devoted some of the best years of his life to unravelling problems arising from Christian Friedrich Matthaei's light-fingered habits in Moscow,[4] and some of Léopold Delisle's friends said that his outstanding accomplishment was his work on the Affaire Libri.[5] A complete bibliography of the reports, pamphlets, and articles about Libri would fill a small volume. The problem of thefts from the open shelves of public libraries is responsible for hundreds of columns of platitudes in the ALA *Proceedings* and the *Library Journal*, although E. W. Gaillard[6] and Isabel Ely Lord[7] have come out with valuable and constructive ideas on this matter. These and other frequently discussed aspects of bibliokleptomania will be given no special treatment here but rather will be dealt with in the same relative proportions as other aspects which have not received exhaustive attention.

The moral questions posed by book theft are considerably more difficult than those involved in deciding the guilt or innocence of a bank robber or kidnapper. Tallemant des Réaux stated categorically in his *Historiettes* that book theft is not true theft if the books are not resold.[8] Hans Bohatta follows substantially the same line of reasoning as Tallemant when he says that book theft proper is taking another's property in order to profit by it, whereas taking a book merely because its possession is coveted belongs more in the realm of bibliomania.[9] However, he does admit that this is a distinction without a difference as far as the victim is concerned. Elsewhere Bohatta states that "The bibliophile is the master of his books, the bibliomaniac their slave."[10] Heinrich Treplin, handling the problem from a purely legal viewpoint,[11] has no difficulty in deciding for himself that without exception any illegal conversion of a movable object, including books, belonging to another, is theft.

The motives of the book thief are as varied as his methods. However, it is possible to divide book thieves into two broad categories, namely, criminals and bibliomaniacs. The criminal steals either from greed or need.[12] Bibliomaniacs may either be private individuals acquiring the books of others for their own collections, or they may be politicians seeking to aggrandize national or university libraries through presenting them with the fruits of conquest or confiscation. Fortunately, the latter type seems to be disappearing, and even the Nazis, for all their reputations as enemies of books, have had relatively few substantiated charges of book theft made against them, at least during the first four years of war. The finest examples of conquerors turned bibliomaniacs belong to the days when wars were fought primarily for territorial gain and considerations of dogma rather than for economic reasons.

This classification of book thieves should not be accepted as hard and fast. Certainly, however, the matter is not so simple as Max Stois would have us believe when he tells us that the only two motives of the book thief are "Gewinnsucht" and "wirkliche Not."[13] The idealistic Bogeng seems inclined to believe that intellectual ambition rather than material covetousness is the primary cause of bibliographical crime.[14] Gaillard points out that in the case of librarians, who are perhaps the most serious offenders, deep-seated motives for theft may be entirely lacking and that thefts by these individuals may often be attributed to the operation of the simple equation Temptation-Opportunity.[15] The complexity of the motivation of a bibliographical criminal is patent to those who wade through the interminable controversies of the Affaire Libri or study the career of T. J. Wise. Sometimes we are inclined to be excessively generous with these individuals simply because such a noble pursuit as book collecting is the ultimate cause of their crime, but it must be admitted that they are nevertheless criminals and, as Bohatta says, it makes little difference to the victim what their motives were.

While there are many bibliomaniacs who are above suspicion as book thieves, Bogeng has struck a note of truth when he remarks that, "There is no deep abyss separating Bibliophile Purgatory from Bibliophile Inferno."[16] An excellent example of a bibliomaniac who slipped from grace is the most famous of his clan, Antoine-Marie-Henri Boulard, a distinguished member of the *corps législatif* during the First Empire. He filled up some five entire houses with from 600,000 to 800,000 volumes, baled or packed in boxes, most of which he had never seen. When the collection was auctioned off in 1828–1833, it played havoc with the Paris market. While virtually everyone who has occasion to mention Boulard dismisses him as a "harmless bibliomaniac," Cim, who had access to many oral or otherwise fugitive traditions of nineteenth-century French bibliophily, offers good evidence to prove that Boulard had "itchy fingers" whenever he saw a volume that could not be bought and excited the acquisitive instincts in him.[17]

Two other types of collectors' and libraries' Nemesis who border on criminality are the absent-minded borrower and the biblioclast. Cim speaks of "emprunteurs indélicats" in very strong terms: "Le fait est que les emprunteurs ont été de tout temps et partout, et bien plus que les rats, les souris, ou les mites, bien plus que l'eau et le feu, la terreur des bibliophiles."[18] Charles Lamb's essay on "The Two Races of Men" (borrowers and lenders) tells how the library of the gentle Elia, whose treasures were "rather cased in leather covers than closed in iron coffers," suffered from the depredations of "those mutilators of collections, spoilers of the symmetry of shelves, and creators of odd volumes." Lucia Borski informs us that in Renaissance Poland the love of books was so great that people sued each other for not returning them.[19] Although the librarian can discipline his delinquent readers with (frequently uncollectable) fines, legal redress is unfortunately seldom available in modern times.

The biblioclast is perhaps even more hateful than the biblioklept, for the result of his work is far more disastrous. The biblioklept will at least save books for posterity, but the biblioclast destroys them forever. Time will heal the ill feeling against Libri, but it can never restore the damage caused by Savonarola's wild mob when it destroyed the Laurentian's copies of Petrarch, Pulci, and other "witty authors" in the religious orgy known as "The Burning of the Vanities." But worst of all is the biblioclast who is also a biblioklept. Andrew Lang felt so strongly about this form of animal life that he created for it the name of "book ghoul."[20] History is full of examples of book ghouls, and the conclusive evidence of their activities is only too often at hand. Cim informs us that a well-known book thief, Dr. R . . . of Lyons, never stole entire volumes but only parts of books with which to complete his own imperfect copies.[21] Firmin Maillard tells the story of a member of the Institute who haunted the shop of Père Lefèvre under the Colbert Arcade of the Bibliothèque Nationale and not only never bought any books from old Lefèvre but actually tore out leaves containing pertinent passages so that he could make notes at his leisure.[22] A similar case occurred at the Iowa State College Library in 1943 when an overly enthusiastic aluminum chemist sabotaged hundreds of irreplaceable serials by tearing out all articles pertinent to his particular investigation.

Perhaps the most curious tale of any book ghoul is that told of Theodor Schwisow by Johannes Lemcke of Hamburg.[23] In 1936 Schwisow was apprehended for book mutilation, and when his quarters were searched incidental to his arrest, hundreds of copper engravings stolen from the libraries at Hamburg and elsewhere were found. He was tried, convicted, and sentenced, but in 1938 he was released from prison. Within two years he was again arrested for stealing copper engravings from the libraries of Hamburg, Rostock, and Göttingen. He had been ordered to replace the prints he had stolen from the Municipal Library at Frankfurt a/M, and this he proposed to do by removing the same prints from copies of the books in other libraries.

It is difficult to believe that the wicked old shoemaker-biblioclast John Bagford was not also a book thief; for in making his *Atlas typographicus* and his collections of paper specimens, bookplates, etc., he certainly must have seen many a volume which he desired but could not purchase. If we are wrong in suggesting that Bagford was a thief, then we are simply making a false conjecture rather than damaging an innocent man because Bagford must surely be sitting in the same corner of bibliographical hell occupied by the Grangerizers and Mathias Flacius (Vlachich). Flacius, the distinguished Lutheran polemicist and historian of the German Reformation, would go to the monasteries disguised as a monk and commit any variety of bibliographical crime which struck his fancy. Preferably he stole the coveted volumes; but whatever was too heavy to take in its entirety he removed with what German bibliophiles bitterly call "das Flacianische Messer" (*cultellus Flacianus*). He would take not only individual leaves but also entire sections. He had a particular taste for engravings.[24]

Repulsive as Flacius is, he is surely a grade higher than the peddlers of initials cut from the parent manuscript. Flacius was at least a creative scholar and saved from oblivion a rich harvest of satirical Latin verse in his *De corrupto Ecclesiae Statu Poemata* (Basel, 1557), but he who strips a manuscript of an initial is taking something which can never be restored. As William Blades remarked, it would seem that the man who cuts an initial from a manuscript is so embittered by the realization that he can't take his library with him to the next world, he is determined to ruin it for his mortal heirs.[25] It may have been ignorance on the part of the choir boys at Lincoln Cathedral who put on their robes in the library and while waiting for the signal to "fall in" amused themselves by cutting out illuminated initials and vignettes;[26] but "Professor Rapisar," who played havoc with some of the Vatican's most valuable illuminated manuscripts, is an entirely different case.[27] One day in the nineties of the last century a "Professor Rapisar" presented himself at the Italian Ministry of Public Instruction in Rome and offered for sale a number of rare miniatures taken from eleventh-century manuscripts. The clerk whom he approached recognized the miniatures as coming from Vatican manuscripts, and he declined the offer and notified appropriate officials in the Papal State at once. Meanwhile it was discovered at the Vatican Library that numerous miniatures were lacking from one especially valuable eleventh-century manuscript. The thief, who turned out to be one Rapisardi from Biancavilla in Sicily, was apprehended, and those miniatures which he had not already sold to second-hand dealers (for a fraction of their true value) were recovered. Some forty-one miniatures had been cut from the eleventh-century manuscript, of which thirty-nine were recovered. He had also cut some seven miniatures from a manuscript of the *Trionfi di Petrarca* as well as a magnificent portrait of Laura (sold in Florence).

The repercussions of this incident were quite serious. For several weeks the Vatican Library was completely shut down, and when it reopened the regulations applying to readers were much more rigid than before. But the most tragic result of the incident was the death of the able prefect of the Vatican Library, Monsignor Isidoro Carini. Carini, supposedly on his way to high places in the Church and an intimate of the Pope, was allegedly reproached severely by the latter for his carelessness in permitting Rapisardi to get away with his bold vandalism. The unfortunate Carini was injured profoundly by the reproach, and it was said that he atoned for Rapisardi's transgressions with his own death. Some said that his demise was the result of a severe stroke caused by his nervous condition, but others argued that it was from poison administered by his own hand. The latter rumor was so strong in the Papal City that the *Osservatore Romano* was compelled to take official cognizance of it.[28]

The history of biblikleptomania goes back to the beginnings of libraries in Western Europe, and undoubtedly it could be traced back even further through the history of Greek and Oriental libraries. Carl Wendel points out that early Roman libraries were largely composed of Greek works simply because the first Roman libraries were stolen from Greece by Roman generals.[29] When Perseus was dethroned, Emilius Paullus took the Royal Macedonian Library as the general's share of the plunder.[30] When Mithridates of Pontos, that most stubborn of the enemies of the Republic, finally succumbed to the forces of M. Licinius Lucullus, the Roman took Mithridates' library and set it up in his plantation at Tusculum where it was freely available to scholars.[31] Another notable example of a Greek library stolen by a Roman general is the collection of Apellicon of Teos, taken by Sulla and later used by Cicero.[32] The more usual type of book thief who makes off with single volumes was also plentiful in Rome. Cicero complains that his trusted slave Dionysius absconded with several valuable manuscripts from his personal collection.[33]

Legend has it that the early Christian communities were also cursed with book thieves.[34] However, "the praiseworthy humility and virtuous tolerance" of St. Anastasius toward a book thief recommends perhaps a bit too much for the present day librarian or bibliophile. Father Anastasius had a complete parchment Bible worth all of eighteen florins which was abstracted from his cell by a lay brother to whom Father Anastasius had shown the volume. While the latter missed the book, he did not have an investigation conducted lest the thief be apprehended and, upon being tried, possibly add to the sin of theft that of perjury. The lay brother went on to the next town and offered the Bible to a prospective buyer for sixteen florins; but the buyer took the book on approval and went to Father Anastasius, the local authority, and asked him for his opinion as to its value. Father Anastasius said merely, "It is a good book and worth the price." When the lay brother was told that Father Anastasius had been consulted and had not exposed him, he was moved to repentance. He withdrew his offer of sale and went forthwith to Father Anastasius with tears in his eyes, begging the saintly man to take his book. At first Father Anastasius refused, but when the lay brother told him his soul would have no peace if he could not get rid of the stolen book, Father Anastasius took it back; but he also took the lay brother into his hermitage, and the two lived together until the Blessed Anastasius passed to his reward.

Lupus of Ferrières was always keenly aware of possible depredations by book thieves, and probably with good reason, for he mentions in a letter to Gottschalk, "The quaternions you found someone had stolen from me . . ."[35] A well-known expression of Lupus' mortal dread of bibliomaniacal hijackers is found in his letter to Hincmar of Rheims who had requested the loan of Bede's commentary:

> I was afraid to send you Bede's commentary on the apostle in accordance with the works of Augustine, because the book is so large that it cannot be hidden in one's cloak, nor comfortably carried in a hand-bag, and even if one or the other could be done, one would have to fear meeting some band of villains whose greed would surely be kindled by the beauty of the manuscript, and it would perhaps be lost thus to both you and me. Accordingly, I can most securely lend the volume to you as soon as, if God will, we can come together at some safe place and will do so.[36]

Book theft was a most serious crime in the eyes of the medieval man. The most effective measure he could think of to protect his books was bibliotaphy, but surely this can be excused as a far lesser sin than book theft, particularly in a day when books were rarer and offered a greater temptation than they do today.[37] Strict loan regulations reminiscent of Lupus' niggardliness, actual concealment of books, and, above all, chaining were the medieval librarian's immediate administrative measures against the book thief. But perhaps the most widely used weapon against book thieves in the Middle Ages was the curse. G. A. Cruewell, who has dealt with this subject exhaustively,[38] has cited numerous examples from oriental manuscripts to show that the curse was not a Christian invention. The first example which he finds in the Western Church is a document relating to a gift of Theotrude to the Abbey of St. Denis in 627. Subsequently the curse gained in popularity as an effective measure against book thieves and continued to be used until the introduction of the printed book. Its disappearance is probably due to the decreased value of books which made their loss somewhat less important and also made them more easily available by honorable means to would-be thieves.

There are innumerable rather quaint examples of the

curse.[39] The monastery of St. Maximin de Micy threatened
the book thief with damnation along with Judas, Ananias,
Caiaphas, and Pilate. The two great medieval schools of writing, the Cistercian monastery at Clairvaux and St. Albans,
specifically invoked anathema. Thus St. Albans manuscripts
frequently end: "Hic est liber sancti Albani quemqui ei abstulerit aut titulum deleverit anathema sit." Most interesting
is a quaint specimen in verse in a breviary now in the library
of Gonville and Caius College, Cambridge:

> Wher so ever y be come over all
> I belonge to the Chapell of Gunvylle hall;
> He shall be cursed by the grate-sentens
> That felonsly faryth and berith me thens.
> And whether he bere me in pooke or sekke,
> For me he shall be hanged by the nekke,
> (I am so well beknown of dyverse men)
> But I be restored theder again.

The express threat of excommunication was not at all un-
common. Cim lists numerous manuscripts containing threats
to excommunicate the thief or to have him stricken from the
Book of Life, and he cites Ludovic Lalanne's authority to
support the tale that in the reading room of the Vatican Library there is a marble tablet on which is inscribed a decree
of Sixtus v excommunicating anyone who removes even a
single book without the Holy Father's permission.[40] Edward
Edwards informs us that as late as 1752 Pope Benedict xiv
issued a bull threatening book thieves with excommunication
in order to protect his Polish library.[41]

Closely related to the curse in medieval manuscripts is the
condemnation of thieves in bookplates.[42] This condemnation
generally takes the form of a fairly gentle warning to potentially delinquent borrowers. Thus David Garrick (who, incidentally, was silly enough to lend his best Shakspere quartos
to the slovenly Samuel Johnson) had an elegant but realistic
quotation from the fourth volume of *Menagiana* on his book-
plate: "La première chose qu'on doit faire quand on a
emprunté un livre, c'est de le lire afin de pouvoir le rendre

plutôt." A much more common and less original admonition
to possible borrower-thieves is: "Gentle reader, take me home;
I belong to John Marks, 20 Cork Street, Cork." Caveats vary
from the gentle reminder of Michael Lilienthal (translated
from the Latin by Hardy):

> Use this book, but let no one misuse it;
> The bee does not stain lilies but only touches them.

to the vigorous uncompromising Renaissance doggerel:

> My Master's name above you se,
> Take heede therefore you steale not mee;
> For if you doe, without delay
> Your necke . . . for me shall pay.
> Looke doune below and you shall see
> The picture of the gallowstree;
> Take heede therefore of thys in time,
> Lest on this tree you highly clime!
> [Drawing of the gallows]

One of the most interesting aspects of book theft in the
Middle Ages is the curious idea of the medieval man that to
borrow a book in manuscript and make an unauthorized copy
of it constituted embezzlement. The most celebrated case of
this type is the quarrel between St. Columba and his teacher,
Finnian of Moville, as related by Adamnan.[43] Columba copied
a psalter which Finnian had lent him, and the latter claimed
not only the original but also the copy as his property. The
dispute became so violent that it was carried to King Diarmid,
who supported the claim of Finnian, saying that the copy
should go with the book "as calf must go with the cow." A
bibliophile of Columba's stature could hardly be expected to
take this Solomonian judgment lying down; and accordingly
he and his followers fought a battle to get back the transcript
and paid for their boldness by being forced into exile.

Joshua Bloch cites rabbinical authority to show that the
scriptural passage, "Men do not despise a thief, if he steal to
satisfy his soul when he is hungry" (Proverbs VI, 30), was
applied to those who stole words of sacred texts by transcrib-

ing them from copies belonging to others.[44] In connection
with his discussion of this matter, Bloch cites from Immanuel
ben Solomon of Rome an interesting tale of two medieval
Jews who fell out because one entrusted his books to the care
of the other, and the latter betrayed his trust by copying some
manuscripts during the former's absence. On the other hand,
Bloch points out that there is considerable evidence to prove
that many Jews were also more than willing to permit their
manuscripts to be copied.

Although books became cheaper with the invention of printing, and as has been pointed out, thus removed some of the
book thief's motivation, the intensified thirst for knowledge
in the Renaissance created new hazards for libraries. In
Bodley's Library even the Benefactors' Register was "cheined
to the deske, at the vpper broad Windowe of the Librarie."[45]
Few scholars who traveled in foreign parts came back with
empty hands.[46] Poggio Bracciolini, who discovered so many
valuable manuscripts in the monasteries of Germany, Switzer-
land, and France, did not always use the most honorable
methods of acquisition; but one is tempted strongly to for-
give almost any bibliographical peccadillo to the savior of
Quintilian, Valerius Flaccus, and Ammianus Marcellinus. As
to his methods, he says of one manuscript: "In manicam
conieci," but we know that he also managed to get hold of
larger ones. Cardinal Bessarion had unusual methods of collecting manuscripts from the moribund Greek monasteries of
Southern Italy of which he was the nominal chief, but Gardthausen excuses him as the rescuer rather than the looter of
the property of these degenerated foundations. When the
riches of the Levantine and other Near Eastern monasteries
were discovered in the first half of the nineteenth century,
much the same type of thing occurred (*infra*).

As we pursue the book thief into modern times, he begins
to assume familiar characteristics and to follow known pat-
terns of behavior (although it must not be assumed that any
criminal specialty ever becomes stereotyped). Book thieves
may now be classified fairly accurately by profession. Head-

ing the list of professions which have produced notable book thieves is that of the librarian. Close on the heels of the librarian come the clergyman and the scholar. As a big operator, the professional thief ranks considerably behind the librarian and the clergyman. Indeed, the librarian rivals the despoiling conqueror and the confiscating revolutionary in the proportions of his thefts. If Count Libri had only been left unmolested a few more years, he might probably have been able to steal as much as had been confiscated during the French Revolution. The two most fearsome book criminals of all, Don Vincente and Pastor Tinius, were Catholic and Protestant clergymen respectively. When we are given an adequate history of Jewish libraries, many a rabbi will probably be exposed and join the ranks of gentile clerical book thieves; and when Indian bibliography progresses beyond its present primeval state, many a *sadhu* will probably be found to have secreted an occasional palm leaf in his loin cloth.

French librarians got the hang of the book theft business not too long after modern libraries began to take form in that country. Pierre de Carcavi, appointed by Colbert as "gardien de la Bibliothèque du Roi," robbed the Bibliothèque Royale of many valuable duplicates.[47] By the nineteenth century Gallic genius had developed book theft into a profession, but it took an Italian to make a fine art of it. Guglielmo Bruto Icilio Timoleone, Conte Libri Carrucci della Sommaia,[48] descendant of the poet Feo della Sommaia who was a friend of both Petrarch and Boccaccio, played such havoc with French libraries in the 1840's that Léopold Delisle was still untangling Libri's obscure cataloguing as late as 1898.[49]

The story of Libri is too well known to repeat in detail. It will be recalled how the young Florentine nobleman held a university degree at the age of seventeen, was professor of mathematics in Pisa at the age of twenty, and was forced to flee to Paris for political reasons before he was thirty (1832). There he soon became famous and influential, winning appointments as professor of mathematics at the Collège de France, chevalier of the Legion of Honor, member of the Institute, editor of the *Journal des Savants*, and inspector in the public school system. He was a well-known figure at the book auctions, and by 1841 his reputation as a bibliophile was enough to justify his appointment as secretary of a commission to make an inventory of the manuscripts in the public (i.e., not private) libraries of France. Immediately he began to "collect"; and although several accusations were made against him early in his career as a book thief, he was protected by the lack of proper cataloguing and the confused political conditions of the day. After a six-year career as a "collector," he decided to have his sale. He auctioned some of his printed books in Paris, but his big haul was the £8,000 he received from Lord Bertram Ashburnham for some 1,923 manuscripts.[50] Unfortunately for Libri, he had been very careless about removing the stamps of some of the victimized French libraries, and the authorities were compelled to take notice. In 1848 he fled to England, taking with him a considerable library which he later auctioned at Sotheby's and Puttick and Simpson, always carefully concealing the provenance of the books and manuscripts and frequently concealing his own connection with the sale. In 1850 he was sentenced *in contumaciam* by a French court to ten years at hard labor. Toward the end of his life he returned to Italy, and in 1869 he died in Fiesole.

The remarkable aspect of the Affaire Libri is not so much the magnitude of the crime as the vehemence of the controversy arising out of it. For ten or fifteen years after his conviction Libri was vigorously defended by such famous names as Gustav Brunet, Laboulaye, Achille Jubinal, Paulin Paris, Paul Lacroix, Guizot, Victor Leclerc, Alfred de Vailly, and Mérimée.[51] Libri cleverly wove into his defense the political troubles arising from the fall of Louis-Philippe. In 1861 he entered an appeal for a reversal of his sentence but was unsuccessful. When Mme. Mélanie Libri, sister of Baron Double, addressed a petition to the French Senate to set aside the judgment in the same year, Attorney General Dupin, already famous as a punster, remarked: "Dans cette affaire

Libri, il y a des gens qui agissent vraiment avec une légèreté de . . . colibri!"[52]
Inseparably connected with the name of Libri is that of Joseph Barrois, one time deputy of the Départment du Nord.[53] After purchasing from Libri a large number of manuscripts which Libri had stolen from the Bibliothèque Nationale, he transported them clandestinely in international commerce from France to England and sold them in 1849 to Ashburnham at the very moment when Libri was being tried in France *in absentia*. Cim argues that Ashburnham was not aware of the source of the manuscripts,[54] but it is difficult to believe that any collector or librarian in Western Europe was not currently posted on the sensational trial resulting from Libri's exposure.

The Libri scandal was one of the favorite topics of conversation of Auguste Harmand, for thirty years municipal librarian at Troyes.[55] Harmand was always delighted to have an opportunity to describe Libri carrying a large brief case and wearing a flowing topcoat in which he would conceal pilfered manuscripts. But not until almost a generation after Libri's depredations had been exposed was it discovered that Harmand was in the same business when the concierge of the library at Troyes caught him in the act of altering the library's stamps. He had covered up his tracks so neatly by removing entries from the catalogue that even Ludovic Lalanne and Anatole de Montaiglon could not find a record that many of the stolen volumes had actually belonged to the library at Troyes. It is interesting to note that Harmand attempted to follow Libri's example for the legal defense of a book thief by attributing his denunciation to political considerations; but he was not quite as successful as his master in the trade, and he was convicted and sentenced to four years in the penitentiary.

German librarians no less than their French confrères have been known to convert feloniously the property in their custody. They range from stack boys[56] to university librarians, and some of their thefts have been almost as significant as Libri's in respect to the scale on which they were conceived.

An important pioneer among German librarian-biblioklepts was Christian Friedrich Matthaei, whose "Drang nach Osten" actually penetrated within the gates of Moscow and netted him at least sixty-one manuscripts taken from various Muscovite libraries.[57]

In 1789 the Russian historian Karamsin was inspecting a Euripides manuscript in the Kurfürstliche (later Königliche, now Staats-) Bibliothek in Dresden. The manuscript looked familiar to him, and knowing that it had been purchased by the library from Matthaei, he was at a loss to figure out where and how the latter had acquired it. But the question as to the provenance of the manuscript remained a mystery for over a century until Oscar von Gebhardt unraveled the whole affair in his brilliant series of articles in the *Zentralblatt für Bibliothekswesen* in 1898. Briefly, the facts of the case are that Matthaei was in Moscow on two occasions, ultimately dying there while occupying the chair of classical philology at the University of Moscow, and that during his first sojourn had held appointments of trust in various Muscovite libraries and had abused his position by committing innumerable thefts. The extent of his depredations has never been ascertained precisely due to the poor state of the catalogues in most of the victimized libraries; but it is known that he sold sixty-one manuscripts to the Kurfürstliche Bibliothek in Dresden and to the university libraries in Leipzig, Leiden, and Göttingen. To Matthaei's credit, it must be stated that his sole motive was not money, but that research problems also entered the picture, for he did not sell the manuscripts until he had exploited them fully. Perhaps for this reason Matthaei had the untidy habit of stealing only portions of manuscripts rather than entire volumes. Accordingly, there arose from this circumstance an Augean stable of confused manuscript pedigrees; but fortunately Gardthausen and Gebhardt have been able to straighten out most of these problems satisfactorily.

German librarians were still considering Russian libraries fair game for booty in the following century; but Alois Pichler[58] was caught in 1871 after having stolen some 4,000 volumes from the Imperial Public Library in St. Petersburg and was sent to Siberia. Pichler was a native of Burgkirchen in Upper Bavaria and had established a solid reputation as a theologian and a classicist before receiving the St. Petersburg appointment. It is of interest to note that when he was apprehended, his thirty-six-year-old female cousin was also taken into custody and sentenced to four months in the workhouse for harboring. This is the only harboring violation in connection with book theft which is known to have been prosecuted, although harboring and receiving are almost as common as the substantive crime. In 1873 Prince Leopold of Bavaria interceded with the Czar on Pichler's behalf, and the librarian was released. He returned to Bavaria where he settled in Siegsdorf near Traunstein, but he died shortly thereafter.

Denmark must share Germany's guilt for producing Daniel Gotthilf Moldenhawer, professor and librarian at both Kiel and Copenhagen in the late eighteenth and early nineteenth centuries.[59] After Moldenhawer's death in 1823 the great bulk of his collection of manuscripts and books, most of which had been acquired by means of which his heirs would not be proud, became a part of the Royal Library in Copenhagen. Moldenhawer made extensive trips all over Europe and spent considerable time in Paris where he investigated the monastic collections. Hans Schulz has cynically but correctly remarked that there is a remarkable correspondence between what Moldenhawer sought in Paris and what his collection was later found to contain.[60]

In spite of the economic distress of post-war Germany, there is but one recorded account of a large scale theft by a librarian, and he an Austrian.[61] Joseph Urdich, a subordinate in the University of Graz Library, was caught because a bank could not understand why such large deposits were being made by an impoverished librarian. Urdich made heavy inroads on an extremely valuable collection of some 20,000 volumes deposited in the basement of the University of Graz Library and not yet catalogued. He covered up his tracks

carefully by falsifying accession entries, substituting uncata-
logued books for catalogued ones and giving them shelf marks
of old ones (another argument in favor of our Anglo-Saxon
"Dogma der systematischen Aufstellung" so bitterly opposed
by many German librarians!). He was no bibliophile. When
he had stolen a book he would invariably tear off the old
binding and replace it with a new one. He was probably one
of the first Austrian Nazis, for when he was unable to eradi-
cate fully all signs of ownership, he would burn the book. On
one occasion his religious scruples hampered his operations.
He had sold a stolen copy of St. Birgitta's *Revelationes*
(Nuremberg, 1500) to a German dealer for RM 300.—, and
the latter had in turn sold it to a Swiss dealer for 15,000
francs. But it was subsequently discovered that the book was
imperfect, and it was returned to the thief. Inasmuch as it
was written by a saint, Urdich hesitated to burn it and therefore returned it to the shelves. Some of Urdich's spoils found
their way to America. One citizen of the United States who
will remain anonymous purchased Konrad Celtes' edition of
Hrotswitha of Gandersheim's *Opera* (Nuremberg, 1501) for
1,650 Austrian shillings.

Other European countries which have produced criminal
librarians in modern times are Italy and Spain. One Passini,
secretary of the University of Parma Library, was jailed in
1885 for stealing 5,000 of the library's 80,000 volumes, among
them numerous early Italian imprints.[62] In Spain the arrest
of one Antonio López-Santos, an employee of the Biblioteca
Nacional in Madrid, and his mistress (named Maria Ma-
dalena!) nearly precipitated a national scandal in 1930.[63]
López-Santos was apprehended after it had been discovered
that he was guilty of stealing certain etchings from the Biblioteca Nacional which subsequently appeared in the possession of a Berlin dealer; and in the search of his quarters made
incidental to his arrest, several valuable works on the conquest
of Peru belonging to the Biblioteca Nacional were also recovered. It was further revealed that López-Santos, supposedly
a poverty-stricken library assistant, had a neat credit of some

RM 80,000.— in a German bank. This scandal was probably responsible for later attacks on Rodríguez Marín, the director of the Biblioteca Nacional, in *El Sol*, liberal Republican paper. Rodríguez, a leading Spanish Germanophile in World War I, at which time he made many enemies, was accused of maladministration and incompetence by *El Sol*.

Private collectors are no more immune to the temptations of books than are librarians. Although it is questionable whether some collectors have been reduced to theft by love of books or money, they have as a class at least produced no such vulgar thieves as Urdich and López-Santos. Among collectors neither age nor rank give immunity to the "amiable weakness" of bibliokleptomania, which claims such eminent victims as Catherine de Medici (who stole Marshal Strozzi's library), Innocent x, Bishop More, and Sir Robert Cotton.[64] The collector stops at nothing to gain his ends, and if we may believe the delightful fiction of Dr. Rosenbach,[65] his ingenuity surpasses that of all other book thieves.

The prototype of the collector-biblioklept is perhaps Sir Edward Fitzgerald.[66] Born of an illustrious English family, wealthy, and with powerful political ties within his family, he started out on a promising diplomatic career which, however, never came to fruition. He began his infamous hobby by stealing books of his friends. On one occasion his wife caught him stealing from the library of a castle in Northumberland and denounced him, but he escaped the net of justice and fled to France. Here his unfortunate passion pursued him, and towards the middle of the nineteenth century he was well known among Parisian *bouquinistes as l'Anglais*. They tolerated his minor depredations on their stock, but one day he overstepped the bounds of their patience when he appropriated a polyglot Bible. He was apprehended and sentenced to two years in the penitentiary.

Perhaps for the very reason that France is the happy hunting ground of the collector and the biblioklept, French librarians have adopted severer administrative measures against thieves than are found in any other country, and likewise

French librarians have shown remarkable ingenuity in protecting their holdings. A particularly sly fellow was Louis Paris, for many years librarian at Rheims.[67] One day he received notice of a prospective visit from M. Béquet, inspector of the University, and Edme Courtois, ex-member of the Convention. Forewarned of Courtois' unenviable reputation as a book thief, Paris resolved to be on his guard during his visit. When they arrived, Paris showed them through his entire library, not omitting the case of incunabula. After a few minutes in the room where the incunabula were shelved, he suddenly noticed that his Lucius Annaeus Florus, which had been in place when they entered, was missing. At first he pretended to take no notice of it, but it was still missing after the tour of the library had been completed. In his despair, Paris turned to his two guests and, frankly declaring himself to be a suspicious man, told them that one of the three—perhaps himself—had stolen the precious volume, and proposed that all three turn their pocket inside out. Paris and Béquet had nothing in their pockets other than the miscellaneous assortment of junk carried by most Frenchmen, but the highly annoyed Courtois was caught red-handed and had to surrender the book to its lawful owner.

Perhaps it is unjust to group clergymen together as a class of book thieves and to rank them second only to librarians in their zeal for their hobby; for, as Pierce Butler indicates[68] in past ages men were churchmen only by convention, actually they were statesmen, legislators, diplomats and administrators. Perhaps one is influenced too much by the tradition of the preacher's son who became the village drunkard or of the divinity student who made bathtub gin in his dormitory room; but the fact remains that clergymen rank high as accomplished book thieves. Out of respect to the cloth we will omit the history of individual biblioklepts in the Middle Ages, virtually all of whom were clerics, and include only those wayward sons of the modern Church who might as well have chosen some other profession to disgrace. In further reverence to the Church it should be emphasized that Innocent x was merely

Cardinal Pamfilio when he first acquired his lifelong grudge against the entire French nation.[69] It began when a Gallic collector detected the future pope abstracting a book from his library and had made so bold as to ask him to put it back. Pamfilio, highly indignant, denied the theft vehemently—so vehemently that the stolen book dropped out from beneath his voluminous cardinal's robes.

One of the most celebrated clerical thieves of the seventeenth century, Jean Aymon,[70] can be blamed on neither the Roman nor the Protestant Church, for he was a renegade in ecclesiastical as well as bibliographical matters. This misguided genius completed his studies for the priesthood under the canonical age, and Innocent xi had to write out a special dispensation for him in which, among other things, the Holy Father said: "Vitae ac morum honestas, aliaque laudabilia probitatis et virtutum merita." Aymon had hardly donned the cloth before he was up to his neck in trouble so serious that he found it expedient to renounce the Church of Rome for a Protestant pastorate in Holland and to break his vow of celibacy and take a wife. But he was no more able to stay out of difficulties in the Protestant Church than he was in the Catholic Church; and accordingly he began to intrigue to return to France and to the bosom of the Church of his fathers. Excluded from France as a Huguenot, he wrote to Nicolas Clément, custodian of the Bibliothèque du Roi in Paris, urging him to intercede in his behalf and at the same time offering for sale the celebrated herbal of Paul Hermann at a bargain price. Fagon, the superintendent of the Jardin Royal, was consulted in the matter of purchasing the Hermann herbal and advised to the contrary; but through further chicaneries, Aymon was able to prevail upon Clément to get him permission to return to Paris. Aymon told the gullible Clément that he had a *magnum opus* to write on the iniquities of the Protestant heretics based on material gathered during his temporary apostasy, and under this pretext he was able to gain entry to the library entrusted to Clément's care. Aymon soon got on Clément's nerves, and the latter was delighted one day

when the renegade failed to show up. But his joy was short
lived, for he soon got a note from a French agent in The
Hague stating that Aymon was in that city attempting to dis-
pose of the precious manuscript of the *Dernier Concile de
Jérusalem tenu par les Grecs au sujet de la transubstantiation*
(1672 and 1673)[71] and several other valuable pieces which
he had feloniously taken from the Bibliothèque du Roi. After
much confusion, many charges and countercharges, Aymon
finally sought a court judgment in The Hague directing the
stolen property to his legal possession; but in 1709 Dutch
justice finally decided that the *Dernier Concile* rightfully belonged in Paris. But in the meanwhile the poor Clément had
had a nervous breakdown and lived only three more years to
enjoy custody of the book. A curious epilogue to Aymon's
thefts is a letter of Philippe de Stosch returning a book stolen
by Aymon from the Bibliothèque du Roi and sold to Stosch
but belatedly recognized.[72]

A Protestant clergyman of the seventeenth century whose
guilt as a book thief has been the subject of considerable
debate was the Dutch philologist Isaak Vossius.[73] Klenz and
other Germans have argued consistently that Vossius stole
not only the Codex Argenteus but also other valuable manuscripts when he parted company with Queen Christina upon
her abdication. But Wieselgren, Grape, and von Friesen argue
that the young queen, unaware of the true value of the Codex
Argenteus inasmuch as her education had been almost exclusively classical, gave it to the Dutchman as a reward for
his services as her librarian and tutor. There is no conclusive
proof to support the arguments of either side; but those who
have seen and admired the Codex Argenteus, aside from its
inestimable philological value, will find it difficult to understand how anyone could willingly part with it. Taken by the
Swedes at Prague in 1648, it became a part of the Queen's
library, but Vossius took it with him when he left Sweden in
1654. In 1662 Count Magnus Gabriel de la Gardie, seventeenth-century Swedish Maecenas, bought it from Vossius and
presented it to the University Library in Uppsala where it is

still retained today.[74] After Vossius died in 1689 in Windsor, where he was a canon, the remainder of Vossius' manuscripts passed to his native city of Leiden.

The eighteenth century produced the most celebrated (and perhaps the least repulsive) of all clerical book thieves, Cardinal Domenico Passionei (1682–1761).[75] Appointed director of the Vatican Library in 1755, he quickly made a reputation for himself by his learning and ability. In Frascati he had his own private collection numbering 60,000 volumes in 1721, not one of which was by a Jesuit. It included the collection of printed books formerly owned by Cassiano del Pozzo and numerous other valuable items whose source was never discussed by Passionei. The facts are that Passionei misused his office in the Church in order to secure books for his private library.[76] When he was in Lucerne as papal nuncio in 1721, he spent much of his time visiting Swiss abbeys, but he rarely left them without looking like a stuffed sausage for all the volumes concealed beneath his flowing cardinal's robes. Or he would inform the prior that he had important researches to make in the library; and, in order "not to be disturbed," he would lock himself in, whereupon he would select the rarest volumes and throw them out of the window to a waiting flunkey. Perhaps because Passionei was so well aware of the possibilities of theft as a means of acquisition, he was extremely careful of his own collection. He described it as his seraglio, and, carrying the figure further, he had the bad taste to call his librarian, none other than Johann Joachim Winckelmann, his eunuch![77] After Passionei's death his collection was sold for 30,000 scudi to the Augustinians, and ultimately it found a home in the Biblioteca Angelica. Cardinal Schiara bought Passionei's prints and presented them to Empress Maria Theresa.

Passionei was not the only Vatican librarian who had an imperfect conception of the laws of "mine" and "thine." On October 13, 1810, Paul-Louis Courier wrote to M. Clavier complaining that Vatican manuscripts "s'en vont tout doucement en Allemagne et en Angleterre."[78] According to Courier, the pillage was begun by one Father Altieri, a Vatican librarian, who sold the manuscripts "comme Sganarelle ses fagots."

Nineteenth-century France produced a clerical book thief ranking second only to Passionei. The Abbé Chavin de Malan[79] operated with the smooth tongue of a confidence man worthy of comparison with Aymon, and soon he won himself a place as the *enfant gâté* of such high prelates as the Archbishop of Paris and the Bishops of Orleans, St. Claude, Langres, and Rennes. With this backing and the excuse that he needed to get at the sources for his *Histoire de Dom Mabillon et de la Congrégation de Saint-Maur*, he was able to prevail on M. Robert, decrepit and complacent director of the Bibliothèque St. Geneviève to give him the key so that he could work there on Sundays. He made good use of his Sabbath labors, at least from his personal standpoint. He was even able to secure the aid of a "commissionaire" to help him cart off the seventeen solidly bound folio volumes of the *Oeuvres* of Denis le Chartreux to his quarters. Altogether the Abbé's *Histoire de Dom Mabillon* cost St. Geneviève some 514 volumes. Later Chavin de Malan turned out to be as great a renegade as Aymon, for he renounced the Church and wed his own cousin. To support his wife he prevailed upon M. de Falloux to get him a job as grand ducal librarian in Luxemburg, but when his wife died he returned to the Church and continued to amuse himself in libraries.

Apropos of the *Histoire de Dom Mabillon* the barefaced Abbé wrote: "Tout l'argent que je pouvais avoir, je l'employais à acheter les ouvrages de Dom Mabillon et de ses confrères; c'était de bien grands sacrifices pour ma pauvre bourse, mais aujourd'hui que je contemple ces chers volumes à leur place d'honneur dans ma bibliothèque, j'ai oublié toutes mes privations . . ."[80] He disposed of the *Oeuvres* of Denis le Chartreux by presenting them to the Abbé Cruice, director of the school of Cannes, but when Cruice discovered their true source he restored them to St. Geneviève. The bulk of Chavin de Malan's collection was purchased by the dealer Demichelis who, in turn, sold the books to the British Museum and American collectors.

Another abbé whom Cim protects with the simple designation of "B . . ." terrorized the *bouqinistes* of the left bank with his thefts around the turn of the century.[81] He was frequently denounced, but he would always become highly indignant, reproaching the poor shopkeeper bitterly for his blasphemously suspicious nature that made him distrust a clergyman. But when he extended his activities to the specimen collection of the École des Mines, positive action was taken by state authorities. His house was raided, the specimens located and returned; and the thief retired to Normandy where he died shortly thereafter.

In nineteenth-century Germany one of the most serious recorded cases of book theft was that of Wilhelm Bruno Lindner,[82] professor of theology in the University of Leipzig and author of several theological works as well as four volumes of poems. His father was the well-known pedagogical theorist Friedrich Wilhelm Lindner. In 1860, twenty-one years after he had received his first appointment on the Leipzig faculty, he was caught in the act of stealing rare books from the University of Leipzig Library. Tried and convicted, he was stripped of his professorship and sentenced to serve six years in the penitentiary, of which he actually served three. In 1876 he died in Leipzig in disgrace.

In the United States, librarians have had a considerable amount of trouble with ministers of the Gospel and with theological students. W. F. Poole remarked that he had been annoyed especially by clergymen who unlawfully coveted the books in libraries of which he was custodian.[83] A. R. Spofford reported that antiquarian dealers in Boston had caught ministers stealing pamphlet sermons and that, as of 1900, the Union Theological Seminary had lost 1,000 volumes.[84] One Funk, a notorious Chicago book thief of the 1880's, went to Cambridge and secured admission to the divinity school, but his record was disclosed when he attempted to get his bond signed, and he committed suicide a few days later.[85] In 1904, Frederick A. Bates, once a minister at Narragansett Pier, R. I., was caught with $3,500 worth of books stolen from the Boston Public Library, Boston University Library, Brown University

Library, Andover Theological Library, the Brockton Public Library, and several others.[86]

The fate of the unhappy Funk suggests that bibilokleptomania may lead to crimes involving considerably greater violence than simple book larceny. Two of the most notorious criminals of the nineteenth century, Johann Georg Tinius, learned German Protestant theologian, and Don Vincente, once a brother of the Cistercian cloister at Poblet (near Tarragona) in Spain, were driven to murder by their insane bibliomania.

Don Vincente[87] once saved the rich library of his cloister from spoliation by robbers by surrendering other treasures to them. Subsequently he appropriated the library for himself and established an antiquarian shop in Barcelona, but he never parted with a valuable book and sold only the less important ones in order to live. It is said that he never read his books. Life might have continued very simply for the renegade, but complications arose in 1836 when the dealer Augustino Patxot outbid him for possession of a copy of Lamberto Palmart's *Furs e ordinacions fetes par los gloriosos reys de Aragon als regnicols del regne de Valencia* (Valencia, 1482), at the time of the sale believed to be a unique copy. The ex-padre grieved so over losing the prize and became so enraged that he murdered Patxot and nine of his customers in order to get possession of this and other books. During the course of the trial Don Vincente became raving mad when he learned that a second copy of the *Furs e ordinacions* had been located in Paris. However, he was found guilty of murder and executed.

Johann Georg Tinius,[88] hero of the Reclam crime thriller, *Der Pfarrer und Magister Tinius, ein Raubmörder aus Büchersammelwut,*[89] became minister in Poserna (near Weissenfels) in 1809. He was twice married, had four children, and led an exemplary personal life. However, in 1813 he was arrested, and after a long drawn out trial he was convicted and sentenced in 1823 to twelve years at hard labor. In spite of his insistent denials, it was proven that he had committed at least two murders in order to secure money to spend on his large private library, variously estimated at from 17,000 to 60,000 volumes. It was sold at a legal auction in 1821. In 1835 Tinius was freed from prison; and in 1846, ostracized by all, he died in Graebensdorf (near Königswusterhausen) where he had been making a living as a hack writer.

Close on the heels of clergymen and occupying third place among biblioklepts are scholars. Indeed, if we take into account the fact that many librarians and clergymen stole books and manuscripts for purposes of research, this category of book thieves may prove to be the largest of all. It should also be noted that frequently the scholar surpasses the iniquities of the biblioklept and reveals himself also as a biblioclast. The excision of encyclopedia articles by readers too indolent to take notes is not a phenomenon restricted to school and public libraries.

One of the earliest of modern scholarly book thieves was Friedrich Lindenbrog (or Lindenbruch)[90] who died in Hamburg in 1648 as a highly respected lawyer. When studying in the Bibliothèque de St. Victor he played havoc with the manuscript collection by indulging in the practice of taking home a manuscript a day and converting it to his own private and exclusive use. Early one morning he was arrested while still in bed (a technique strikingly similar to modern police raids), but he was freed a few days later when Pierre Dupuy (Puteanus) vouched for him. Klenz, in justice to Lindenbrog, notes that some sources attribute this story not to Friedrich Lindenbrog but rather to his older brother, Heinrich, who died in 1642 while serving as librarian at Gottorp.

Perhaps the most delightful tale in the annals of book theft is that of a friend of Diderot whom the encyclopedist chose to call "le petit Chose."[91] "Le petit Chose" was in fact a little man who had had the good fortune to meet the famous writer; and in order to curry favor with the great man, he regaled him with gifts of rare and valuable books. Diderot accepted them and was rather proud to display them to his friends, but he was puzzled as to their origin. After questioning "le petit Chose" in detail, he finally discovered that they were stolen. Diderot insisted that the little man return them to their proper owners; but the latter informed the encyclopedist that this was impossible inasmuch as the books had belonged to the Abbé de Gatient, a canon of Notre Dame who had died a few days previously and whose library had been placed under seal. "Le petit Chose" had been the Abbé's secretary. Naturally, Diderot attempted to restore the books to the heir of the Abbé de Gatient, but when the heir was located, he refused to accept the books. Diderot was compelled to retain them, and with them he kept "le petit Chose" as his librarian. The latter cared for the collection until it finally passed into the hands of Catherine the Great.

One of the most fruitful sources for accessions of nineteenth-century European libraries were the "explorations" of the Near East. In the interests of bibliographical piety it might be well not to go too deeply into the careers of Baron Tischendorf, Henry Tattam, and other explorers of the Levant and the Near East, for there are already a sufficient number of manuscript thieves in these regions convicted by history. Perhaps most notorious of all was the Russian Bishop Porfyrii Uspenskij,[92] who is definitely known to have committed the grossest abuse of the confidence of some of his orthodox coreligionists. Strzygowski states that anyone who has followed Uspenskij's trail in the Near East will find numerous mutilated manuscripts which might be completed from fragments preserved in the Public Library of St. Petersburg (Leningrad). A great scandal was caused among Byzantinists in 1899 when a precious gospel of John Keliot preserved among the relics (not in the library) of the Pantokrator Monastery on Mount Athos disappeared. Only after a long search was it discovered that it had been sold in Athens; and so indignant was the Patraiarchal Synod in Constantinople that it roused itself sufficiently to have the culprit punished.[93] Authorized agents of occidental libraries have also committed grave breaches of propriety in the Near Eastern monasteries. There are uncomplimentary rumors concerning the legitimacy of the means used by the famed Egyptologist Heinrich Karl Brugsch in "collecting" from the Sinai region manuscripts which were ultimately acquired by the Preussische National- (Königliche) Bibliothek in 1866.[94] Considerably more slippery than Brugsch was one Minoïde Mynas,[95] a Greek either by birth or by profession, who was commissioned by the French government to visit certain Levantine monasteries. He brought back numerous important manuscripts, among others the fables of Babrius and a treatise by Philostratus. These two, however, he did not turn over to the French government but sold to the British Museum, which according to Maillard, purchased them with guilty knowledge.

Toward the latter part of the nineteenth century Italy was particularly cursed by book thieves. Not only Libri, Passini, and Rapisardi illuminate the annals of book theft in Italy, but also there have been several Germans accused by the Italians of violating the hospitality of Italian libraries. Most notorious of all was the case of Gustav Hänel,[96] distinguished professor of law at Leipzig who died in 1878 and left his fine legal collection to the University of Leipzig Library. Federico Patetta accused Hänel of having committed a *fatto turpe* in the acquisition of the valuable Codex Utinensis, but R. Helssig defended Hänel ably and even tried to prove that Patetta had made his charges in a fit of nationalistically charged rage. Patetta answered with a flat denial of Helssig's implications and demanded the return of the Codex Utinensis. Further exchanges of notes degenerated into an academic squabble.

The continent proper was not the only haunt of scholarly book thieves. M. Hyamson tells the story of how as a youth he was sent to catalogue a library which had been bequeathed to a public institution in England, only to discover upon his arrival that a noted scholar, a friend of the deceased, was calmly writing his name into every volume of any possible interest to him.[97] Pittolet reported that a twenty-eight-year-old student named Samuel Lavega Santo Tomás working in the Biblioteca de San Isidro stole in whole or in part all the sources for his dissertation on Roman sarcophagi.[98] The most amusing book theft of modern times occurred during the last days of St. Petersburg.[99] It seems that a noted Jewish scholar who had worked for long years in the Asiatic Division of the Imperial Public Library had been caught in the act of stealing certain valuable manuscripts. It was late in the last war, and the Kaiser's armies were battering at the gates of Courland and Ingermannland; but Czarist justice shook off its lethargy, arrested and indicted the subject and brought him to trial. On the stand as a witness in his own defense he argued that it was absurd to charge him, a respectable patron for thirty years, with theft and that even if he had stolen anything, then the fact that the librarians were so careless as to allow him to get away with it justified leaving in his custody any such stolen property, for he could take far better care of it. He was acquitted.

Some of the thieves discussed in the preceding pages have stolen primarily out of the desire for personal gain, but most of them have at least had some pretense to a higher reason for acquiring specific books. While librarians, theologians, and scholars may frequently have more laudable purposes than the common thief, the latter exercises greater care in preserving intact the physical entity of the book, which to him is a matter of dollars and cents.[100] Nevertheless, a thief with no intellectual pretensions is in general considered to be on a lower level than his confrères with doctoral titles.[101] In the early 1900's there was M. Thomas, chevalier of the Legion of Honor, who had access to the Lesoufaché Collection of the Bibliothèque de l'École des Beaux Arts by virtue of his position as government architect and stole from it hundreds of volumes which he subsequently sold in Germany.[102] Thomas was a scoundrel in other aspects as well. He had been deprived of his position as architect of the Grand Palais because of obvious errors in his work, although he had been allowed to retain a similar position with the National Archives. In the latter capacity he stole hundreds of ancient carvings, pieces of ironwork, and other *objets d'art* and converted them to his own private use in his chateau in Sologne. Friedrich Viktor Loth,[103] with aliases, a Prussian "Referendar," stole books around the turn of the century from German libraries. He was actuated by motives no more edifying than those of Thomas. He was accustomed to go to the University of Leipzig Library, register under the name of O. Peters, and conceal books on his person at the opportune moment. In the search of his quarters (rented under the name of Dr. Röder) incidental to his arrest it was revealed that he had also robbed the University of Halle Library (using the alias of Rother), the library of the Leipzig Bar Association, and the Leipzig Chamber of Commerce Library (as Dr. phil. O. Schröder). About the same time that Loth was active one Berthel[104] was stealing many valuable items from the Bibliothèque Royale in Brussels and selling them to German dealers. However, one Munich dealer refused to allow Berthel to dupe him into buying stolen property; and when the latter offered for sale books which were known to exist only in Brussels, he immediately notified officials of the Bibliothèque Royale. Librarians in Brussels were able to identify the thief in short order and take appropriate steps to put a stop to his activities.

One of the most notorious bibilographical scandals of the nineteenth century was due apparently to some common thief who was able to get at the treasures of the Biblioteca Columbina in Seville.[105] This once noble collection was started by Fernando Columbus, son of the Admiral, who collected books and manuscripts throughout the Netherlands, France, England, and Spain. In due time this collection of some 15,000 to 20,000 items was incorporated as the Biblioteca Colombina in Seville. It grew slowly, for biblioklepts nibbled at it constantly and stunted its growth. Accordingly, it is no surprise when we note that in 1870 the Biblioteca Colombina had barely tripled its original size. About this time the thefts increased at a rapid pace, and in the winter of 1885 and 1886 large quantities of *cosas de España* traceable to the Colombina began appearing in the second-hand shops and on the auction blocks of Paris. The name of the thief was never disclosed, but on the basis of a careful investigation it was surmised that he was some individual who had complete and unhampered access to the shelves. Hartwig published an enlightening although somewhat sarcastic reaction to the whole affair. He bitterly remarked that the prelates of the Cathedral in Seville would not honor a formal request from a respected German scholar for international interlibrary loan of a manuscript but paid so little attention to their treasures in their own country that a thief was able to remove them by the crate.[106]

A curious twist in the annals of book larceny occasioned by the lush twenties (and its bumper crop of confidence men) has been analyzed by John T. Winterich.[107] Pointing at the resurgence of interest in Americana, he emphasized the increased danger to public libraries which were keeping on open shelves thousands of valuable Americana which had been little more than booksellers' plugs a generation previously. Even a near illiterate could learn the few basic rules for priority of printing and be fully equipped to despoil small public libraries of unrecognized treasures on their shelves. Winterich is perhaps too charitable in excusing librarians for not being diagnosticians of rare book values. Many choice items might be enjoying a better fate today if our library schools had given a bit more instruction in this type of diagnostics.

Perhaps the most sensational book thief of the 1920's in America was one Joseph Francis de Vallières d'Or, "M. D."[108] Claiming to be the heir to three unsettled English estates, he rented the residence of General David L. Brainerd at 1825 Q Street, Washington, D. C., in 1922. On January 2, 1924, he folded up his tent and stole away—with some 500 rare and valuable books and manuscripts from the General's private collection together with engraved plates from other books and even a few original paintings stripped from their frames. Upon discovering his loss, General Brainerd immediately printed a notice in *Publishers' Weekly* urging dealers to be on the lookout for his property. Six months later a young woman appeared at William J. Campbell's office in Philadelphia offering for sale certain autographs of Washington, Franklin, and Burns, and watercolor sketches signed by John Trumbull, all of which were immediately recognized by Mr. Campbell's son,

John J. Campbell, as the missing property of General Brainerd. It turned out that the young woman was the innocent tool of the thief who, under his alias of "Dr. d'Or" had hired her as a "bookkeeper" and included among her duties the disposal of the stolen property, explaining that he had inherited it. "Dr. d'Or" was subsequently apprehended on the basis of information supplied by the young woman.

The Great Depression of 1929–1941 was highly productive of book thieves. On several occasions *Publishers' Weekly* printed strong editorials pointing out the seriousness of certain thefts and urging libraries to place more restrictions on the use of rare and valuable books. In 1936 especial indignation was expressed at recent thefts of books valued at from $25,000 to $40,000 from the Library of Congress and other libraries.[109] In 1937 a Newark secondhand dealer was found in the possession of large numbers of books stolen during the preceding four or five years from various public libraries in New England and New Jersey.[110] It was pointed out that although the books had evidently passed through the hands of several owners before reaching the Newark dealer, no one seemed to have recognized them for library property or as being of any special value. Yet nearly all still had the marks of ownership intact, and a number of them were first editions of New England poets.

Particularly notorious among the thieves of the Depression was "Dr." Harold B. Clarke, with aliases Gordon Forrest and Rodney Livingston.[111] On June 8, 1931, he was apprehended in a hotel room in Revere, Massachusetts, that looked like a bookbinder's workshop. At the time of his arrest he was found busily engaged in the obliteration of the marks of ownership of the libraries he had victimized. Some thirty American first editions and Western Americana were recovered in his room. He confessed to having stolen some $8,000 worth of books from the Harvard College Library; and in his confession he included fantastic tales about a gigantic ring of book thieves whose actual existence was never proven. Another serious offender was Stanley Wemyss, apprehended on September 21,

1936, as a result of the work of William Mahony, special investigator of the Newark Public Library.[112] Wemyss had stolen three rare pamphlets valued at $50 from the Newark Public Library. After three unsuccessful attempts at suicide, he finally confessed to an eight-year-old career as a book thief in public, university and research libraries. A serious case in 1937 was that of eighty-four-year-old Dr. Milton Miller of Philadelphia, an alumnus of the University of Pennsylvania, who stole some 175 volumes from the University of Pennsylvania Library and from the Mercantile and Free Libraries of Philadelphia.[113] He was caught when he offered ten books for sale to Richard Wormser, who noticed the library marks and reported the matter to the police.

In the United States today the most serious error a book thief can make is to steal books or manuscripts worth $5,000 or more and transport them across a state line. Such a crime constitutes a violation of the National Stolen Property Act, and to violate this statute will set the FBI as well as local peace officers on the trail of the biblioklept.[114] Evidently this statute was unknown to William John Kwiatowski, with aliases Thomas E. Cleary, William Potter, William Johnson, Elmer Potter, Walter Grelanka, Edgar Guest, Dr. Kent, H. Thompson Rich, William Cleary, George Kock, and Douglas Coleman,[115] and his accomplices, Edward Walter Kwiatowski (his brother), Joseph Biernat (his brother-in-law), and Donald Lynch, with alias Professor Sinclair E. Gillingham, when they engineered the theft of the Chapin Library's first folio on February 8, 1940.[116] The Kwiatowski brothers and their brother-in-law, Biernat, prevailed upon thirty-six-year-old Lynch to dye his hair gray, forge a letter of introduction from the president of Middlebury College, and assume the alias of Professor Sinclair E. Gillingham. Lynch successfully carried out his rôle, gained admission to the Chapin Library, and, using the ruse of substitution employed by Dr. Rosenbach's thief of *The Unpublishable Memoirs*, got possession of the coveted folio. Lynch had been promised an even $1,000 for his part in the job, but his niggardly accomplices doled him out only enough to keep him quiet. Beset by domestic troubles, Lynch took to strong drink to forget his difficulties; and on June 30, 1940, while resting in the arms of Bacchus in an Albany, New York, bar, he was arrested for drunkenness. Taken to the station, Lynch bitterly confessed his part in the crime and exposed the Kwiatowskis and Biernat.

FBI agents conducted an investigation to corroborate Lynch's confession, and on July 7, 1940, they arrested William John Kwiatowski, Edward Walter Kwiatowski, and Joseph Biernat and searched their homes. William John was not located at first, but persevering agents finally pulled him out from under a pile of laundry in the corner of a closet in his parents' home. The missing folio was not located in the course of the search, but other valuable books stolen from various libraries were found and returned to their respective owners. The thieves vigorously denied their guilt, but nevertheless they were indicted by a Federal grand jury on September 12, 1940. Prior to the return of the indictment, however, the defense attorney appeared in the office of the United States Attorney in Albany, New York, and reported that one morning when he came to work he found the missing folio on his desk. He stated that he had no idea of how it had found its way to his office but that he did want to surrender it to the government for return to Williams College. Less than a month after the indictment was returned the defendants were arraigned before United States District Judge Harold Burke at Rochester, New York. Edward Walter and William John Kwiatowski were sentenced to two years, Joseph Biernat to eighteen months, and Donald Lynch to three months in a Federal penitentiary designated by the Attorney General.[117]

The device of substitution was about the only feasible one for removing such a bulky tome as a first folio. However, thefts of an even more monumental nature (in regard to size) have been recorded. It is said that during the 1920's a certain rabbi clothed in the flowing robes still used by Eastern European Jews was able to cart off in a few hauls the entire *Jewish Encyclopaedia* owned by the American Library in Paris. Cim cites other examples of the difficult science of purloining heavy references works in many volumes.[118] Gaillard reports that one bookseller lost several copies of *Webster's International Dictionary* in a single afternoon.[119] In the matter of numbers of volumes stolen by any one individual, there have probably been few thieves who have surpassed the totals of Libri, Pichler, and Passini. Possibly worth mentioning, however, is the thief who took 1,500 volumes from the Worcester Public Library[120] and the one who removed 1,000 from the University of Aberdeen Library between 1933 and 1936.[121]

The literature dealing with the problem of theft in public libraries is far too voluminous to discuss in detail here. Fundamentally, theft in public libraries is an administrative rather than a bibliographical problem. It is not likely that theft from a public library will cause as much grief in straightening out manuscript pedigrees as did the thefts of Libri and Matthaei. The basic studies for an introduction to the problem of theft in public libraries are Gaillard's article on "The Book Larceny Problem,"[122] and Isabel Ely Lord's speech at the Minnetonka Conference of the ALA on the question of "Open Shelves and the Loss of Books."[123] One rather interesting device of public libraries to get back books from non-willful delinquents is the "Conscience Week."[124] Some private collectors with forgetful *amici* might well consider the adoption of a similar policy.

From the standpoint of the prevention of book theft one of the most serious obstacles is the unwillingness of libraries to prosecute known thieves.[125] Many college and public libraries boldly post the state statutes protecting their property; yet when they catch a thief, they are afraid to prosecute him for fear of the unfavorable publicity to which they might be exposed. Exit control is the most prevalent device for prevention today, and it is used by many small public libraries as well as large research libraries.[126] Many libraries follow the practice of placing their stamp on a certain fixed page of each book so that if that page is mutilated by eradication of the stamp or perforation, the book can still be identified as the property of a particular library. Thus any book whose page 97 shows signs of tampering most probably belongs to the Bibliothèque Nationale or to the Brooklyn Public Library. Cim cites the case of the clever young man who appropriated an engineering treatise from St. Geneviève and carefully removed the stamp from the usual position on page 41; but unfortunately for him, it was a two volume work bound in one, and he forgot page 41 of volume ii.[127] Unquestionably the most effective device for protecting a library was the practice of a Hague collector who was ever happy to show his collection of Elzevirs but insisted that all visitors put on a full length robe without sleeves or any other apertures.[128]

Book thieves prefer libraries to bookstores as the scene of their operations principally because the danger is less, although there are several other factors at work such as the greater susceptibility of the librarian to the confidence man, the greater accessibility of the books, and the wider variety which is available. But there have also been many accomplished operators in the bookstores. Paris seems to be one of their favorite haunts.[129] One nineteenth-century Parisian book thief became such a well-known nuisance among the *bouquinistes* that they got together and refused to tolerate him any longer. Accordingly, on the day after each "successful" theft he would receive a bill from his victim setting forth author, title, and price of the missing book. At the Hôtel des Ventes he would be stopped at the door and asked whether or not he had taken this or that volume "by error." "Ma foi, oui!" was the invariable and always unembarrassed reply, and the volumes(s) would be immediately and unceremoniously restored. One worthy female devotee of Paul Bourget who apparently lacked either the means or desire to buy this author's works became known among the dealers on the left bank as "la dame au parapluie" for her unusual place of concealment. Again there was a hunchback who cultivated a passion for first editions of novels. He would drop his cane in the expectancy that it would be picked up in deference to his affliction; and as the clerk leaned over to retrieve it, the hunchback would slip several desired firsts into his portfolio.

An old trick in the book stores is to present a priced book to the cashier claiming it came from the three-for-a-quarter counter. Some of the higher class confidence men can get away with this. Somewhat less worthy is the device of sending the clerk to the rear of the shop while the patron helps himself to the books shelved in the front.

One aspect of book theft which has been mentioned in passing is the matter of confiscation by the state, either in the course of conquest or of revolution. Confiscation has been such an important means of acquisition for libraries in the past that a full discussion of this topic belongs in reality to the history of libraries. In modern Europe there has been so much confiscation by national governments that any attempt to restore all books and manuscripts to their original owners would amount to a veritable migration of the peoples.

It has already been noted that early Roman libraries were almost invariably stolen from Greece by Roman generals. This custom was one of the first lessons learned by the Renaissance from antiquity. Catherine de Medici revealed few scruples in taking Marshal Strozzi's library. The Royal Library in Stockholm acquired its most notable treasures as the result of Swedish campaigns in Germany, Denmark, Poland, Bohemia, and Moravia during the Thirty Years' War.[130] His Protestant Swedish Majesty robbed every cloister or Jesuit College of any item whatsoever to which he attached the slightest value and sent it back to Sweden. Thus the famed Codex Giganteus ("Gigas Librorum") in the Royal Library and the Codex Argenteus were originally acquired in this manner. On the other hand, the collections robbed from Würzburg (1631), Olmütz (1642), Nikolsburg (1649), and Prague (1648) were subsequently taken out of the country by Queen Christina upon her abdication and are now in the Biblioteca Reginae in Rome.

The great raids on the ecclesiastical libraries began in the latter part of the eighteenth century and lasted for over a hundred years. Upon the expulsion of the Jesuits from Bavaria the Königliche (now Staats-) Bibliothek was considered enlarged by the addition of the books from the suppressed houses; and to add insult to injury, the collection was moved in 1784 to the building once occupied by the Jesuit College. Again in the nineteenth century this same library enjoyed tremendous gains resulting from the secularization of monastic collections. The Vienna K. K. Hof- (now National-) Bibliothek acquired many of its rarities during the reign of Joseph ii by the addition of monastic collections from Styria, Carinthia, and Tyrol. In 1835 monastic property throughout Portugal was nationalized, and the books and manuscripts were divided among the National Library in Lisbon, the Oporto Library, the Evora Library, and the University of Coimbra Library.[131] Unfortunately, these acquisitions are still to be catalogued satisfactorily, and numerous manuscripts in Portuguese libraries are crying for collation and editing.

But no library in Europe has ever profited from confiscation as much as the Bibliothèque Nationale and other Parisian state libraries during the French Revolution. Much of the credit for saving the books from the dissolved monasteries from destruction is due to H. P. Ameilhon, librarian of the Arsenal, who was instrumental in organizing a commission to group and allocate the libraries taken from the monasteries. During the Revolution the Bibliothèque Nationale doubled within a few years by the addition of libraries of émigrés and suppressed ecclesiastical foundations. The Mazarine is said to have added some 50,000 volumes taken from the monasteries. During the Napoleonic wars the policy of confiscation was extended to other countries, but at Vienna in 1815 the French were made to return all the books stolen by their emperor. Until Amgot gives us an authoritative report, we cannot be sure of what the Nazi have stolen in the present war. It is said that they have raided the Royal Library in The Hague and the Turgenev Library in Paris, but no unequivocable proof is available.

Libraries and nations have long memories about confiscations. The Imperial Public Library at St. Petersburg was greatly enriched in 1794 by the addition of 250,000 books and 10,000 manuscripts from the Zaluski Library in Warsaw, all

stolen by General Suvarof.[132] But under the Treaty of Riga
in 1920 the Bolsheviks were compelled to make good the mis-
deeds of the Czars over a century previously and return the
stolen books. In our own country many Southern state archives
are said to have been indiscriminately plundered by carpet-
baggers during the Reconstruction; and as late as 1912 the
Virginia State Library was able to identify as its property
many items from the Benson J. Lossing collection of manuscripts then being offered for sale by the Anderson Galleries.[133]

Notes . . .

1. Quoted by Ludwig Traube in *Vorlesungen und Abhandlun-
gen*. Munich: C. H. Beck, 1909–1920, i, p. 39.
2. Paris: H. Daragon, 1903.
3. Weimar: Gesellschaft der Bibliophilen, 1915. i, p. 158–212.
4. *Katalog der griechischen Handschriften der Universitäts-
Bibliothek zu Leipzig*. Leipzig: Otto Harrassowitz, 1898; *Katalog
der Handschriften der Universitäts-Bibliothek zu Leipzig*, vol. iii,
reviewed by Karl Krumbacher in the *Byzantinische Zeitschrift*, vii,
1898, p. 626.
5. *Les manuscrits des fonds Libri et Barrois, rapport adressé à
M. le Ministre de l'instruction publique, des cultes et des beaux-
arts*. Paris: H. Champion, 1888.
6. "The Book Larceny Problem," *Library Journal*, xlv, 1920, p.
247–254, 307–312.
7. "Open Shelves and the Loss of Books," *Bulletin of the American Library Association*, ii, 1908, p. 231–253. (Discussion, p.
253–254).
8. Bogeng, *Die grossen Bibliophilen; Geschichten der Bücher-
sammler und ihrer Sammlungen*. Leipzig: E. A. Seemann, 1922.
i, p. 501; Max Sander, "Bibliomania," *Journal of Criminal Law
and Criminology*, xxxi, 1943, p. 160.
9. "Bücherdiebstahl," in Karl Loeffler and Joachim Kirchner, ed.,
Lexikon des gesamten Buchwesens. Leipzig: Karl W. Hiersemann,
1935–1937, i, p. 296.
10. "Bibliomanie," ibid., i, p. 195–196.
11. "Das Bibliotheksrecht," p. 609, in Fritz Milkau and Georg

Leyh, eds., *Handbuch der Bibliothekswissenschaft.* Leipzig: Otto Harrassowitz, 1931–1940, II, p. 599–634.

12. Cim, *op. cit.,* p. 62–105, lists Aymon, Libri, and Harmand among those whose sole or chief motive was monetary gain, but his judgment is debatable in each of these cases.

13. "Das gestohlene Buch," *Zentralblatt für Bibliothekswesen,* XLIV, 1927, p. 174.

14. *Die grossen Bibliophilen,* I, p. 502.

15. *op. cit.,* p. 253–254. Another interesting finding by Gaillard is his correlation of delinquent fines (and subsequent loss of the borrowing privilege) with the rate of theft in public libraries.

16. *Streifzüge eines Bücherfreundes,* I, p. 168.

17. *op. cit.,* p. 21–23. Bogeng, *Die grossen Bibliophilen,* I, p. 500, considers Boulard to be quite harmless. See also Sander, op. cit., p. 160–161, for an amusing account of Boulard. There is no evidence to indicate that Boulard's Anglo-Saxon counterpart, Richard Heber, was not always very scrupulous in his methods of acquisition.

18. *op. cit.,* p. 3.

19. "A Short History of Printing in Poland," *Bulletin of The New York Public Library,* XLVII, 1943, p. 84.

20. *The Library.* London: Macmillan, 1892. 2nd ed. p. 56–57.

21. *op. cit.,* p. 51.

22. *Les passionés du livre.* Paris: Émile Rondeau, 1896. p. 6–7. Maillard (p. 7) also tells the story of MM. de Quatremère, perhaps not thieves but surely among the most reprehensible of biblioclasts. They tore up twenty copies of one rare book in order to complete a single imperfect copy.

23. Bücherdiebstahl," *Zentralblatt für Bibliothekswesen,* LV, 1938, p. 375; and a note in the section entitled "Kleine Mitteilungen," *ibid.,* LVII, 1940, p. 359.

24. Heinrich Klenz, "Gelehrten-Kuriositäten. I. Büchernarren und gelehrte Bücherdiebe," *Zeitschrift für Bücherfreunde,* N. F., V, 1913, p. 49–54; Ernest P. Goldschmidt, *Medieval Texts and Their First Appearance in Print.* London: The Bibliographical Society, 1943; *Supplement to the Bibliographical Society's Transactions,* no. 16, p. 39, 77–79.

25. *The Enemies of Books.* London: Elliot Stock, 1902. Rev. and enl. ed. p. 120.

26. *ibid.,* p. 115–116.

27. Note in the section entitled "Mittheilungen aus und über Bibliotheken," *Zentralblatt für Bibliothekswesen,* XII, 1895, p. 136–137.

28. O. H[artwig], "Monsignor Isidoro Carini," *Zentralblatt für*

Bibliothekswesen, xɪɪ, 1895, p. 198–200, and Léon Dorez, "'Mgr Isidoro Carini, Préfet de la Bibliothèque Vaticane," *Revue des Bibliothèques*, 1, 1895, p. 83. Gallic delicacy (if not piety) forbade Dorez to mention the circumstances of Carini's death.

29. "Das griechisch-römische Altertum," p. 33–35, in *Handbuch der Bibliothekswissenschaft*, ɪɪɪ, p. 1–63.

30. "Stealing a Whole Library," *Publishers' Weekly*, cvɪ, 1924, p. 970–971.

31. Wendel, *loc. cit.*; Plutarch, *Lucullus*, xLɪɪ; Isidore, *Etymologiae*, vɪ, sec. 5, 9.

32. Wendel, *loc. cit.*; J. W. Thompson, *Ancient Libraries*. Berkeley, California: University of California Press, 1940. p. 28–30. The library originally belonged to Aristotle.

33. *Ad fam.* xɪɪɪ, 77.

34. *The Legend of Saint Anastasius*, translated from the German by Theodore W. Koch. Evanston, Ill.: Charles Deering Library, Northwestern University, 1938. "Reprinted from The Northwestern University Alumni News, January, 1938."

35. *Ep.* Lxxɪɪɪ: 145. *Cited in* J. W. Thompson, *The Medieval Library*. Chicago: The University of Chicago Press, 1939. p. 98–99. See also Ludovic Lalanne, *Curiosités bibliographiques*. Paris: Paulin, 1845; *Bibliothèque de la poche*, no. 3, p. 41.

36. *Ep.* Lxxxv: 160–161. Cited in Thompson, *The Medieval Library*, p. 97.

37. Bogeng, *Die grossen Bibliophilen*, ɪ, p. 503.

38. "Die Verfluchung des Bücherdiebes," *Archiv für Kulturgeschichte,* ɪv, 1906, p. 197–223.

39. Examples noted in this paragraph are taken from John W. Clark, *The Care of Books*. Cambridge: The University Press, 1901. p. 77–79.

40. *op. cit.*, p. 63–65.

41. *Memoirs of Libraries*. London: Trübner & Co., 1859. ɪɪ, p. 547 (note).

42. For a full discussion of this matter see W. J. Hardy, *Bookplates*. London: Kegan Paul, Trench, Trübner & Co., 1897, 2nd ed. p. 162–177. The material contained in this paragraph is taken from Hardy.

43. Karl Christ, "Das Mittelalter," p. 119, in *Handbuch der Bibliothekswissenschaft*, ɪɪɪ, p. 90–285, and Ernest A. Savage, *The Story of Libraries and Book-Collecting*. London: George Routledge & Sons, n. d., p. 43–44. Savage thinks that the volume in question was the *Leabhar Cathach* ("Book of Battle"), now in the possession of the Irish Academy.

44. "The People and the Book; on the Love, Care and Use of

Books among the Jews," p. 305–307, in Deoch Fulton, ed., *Bookmen's Holiday: Notes and Studies Written and Gathered in Tribute to Harry Miller Lydenberg.* New York: The New York Public Library, 1943. p. 275–315.
45. Quoted from the Statutes. See *Trecentale Bodleianum.* Oxford: At the Clarendon Press, 1913. p. 34.
46. There is a good treatment of this matter in Viktor Gardthausen, *Handbuch der wissenschaftlichen Bibliothekskunde.* Leipzig: Quelle & Meyer, 1920. I, p. 177.
47. Cim, *op. cit.*, p. 65–66.
48. There is a good introductory bibliography on the enormous mass of Libri literature in Bogeng, *Die grossen Bibloiphilen,* III, p. 246–247. The basic document in the Affaire Libri is Léopold Delisle's *Les manuscrits des fonds Libri et Barrois.*
49. "Les vols de Libri au Séminaire d'Autun," *Bibliothèque de l'École des chartes,* LIX, 1898, p. 379–392.
50. For a concise account of Ashburnham's relations with Libri see Seymour de Ricci, *English Collectors of Books and Manuscripts (1530–1930) and Their Marks of Owenership.* Cambridge: The University Press, 1930. p. 131–138. The great bulk of the Ashburnham manuscripts, excepting only the 996 items in the Stowe Collection, were stolen property. In addition to his large purchase from Libri, Ashburnham paid Joseph Barrois *(infra)* £6,000 for 702 stolen items in 1849. When Ashburnham died, his heirs found few libraries willing to purchase manuscripts with such shady pedigrees. The Libri manuscripts ultimately went back to Paris and to Italy; but most of the Barrois manuscripts were not sold until 1901, when Sotheby disposed of them for over £26,000 to the Bibliothèque Nationale, the British Museum, the Boston Public Library, and the Morgan, Walters, and Fairfax Murray Collections.
51. Cim, *op. cit.*, p. 81.
52. *ibid.*, p. 89–90.
53. Delisle, *Les manuscrits des fonds Libri et Barrois;* Bogeng, *Die grossen Bibliophilen,* I, p. 458, and III, p. 224–225 (bibliography); De Ricci, *loc cit.*
54. *op. cit.*, p. 93, note 1.
55. The best discussions of Harmand's activities are found in Maillard, *op. cit.*, p. 115–120, and Cim, *op. cit.*, p. 94–98.
56. A brief note in the column "Mitteilungen aus und über Bibliotheken" in the *Zentralblatt für Bibilothekswesen,* XVIII, 1901, p. 183, informs that a stack boy in the Buchgewerbemuseum in Leipzig, was given two weeks in the workhouse for six thefts.
57. The complete account of Matthaei's activties has been worked out by Oscar von Gebhardt, "Christian Friedrich Matthaei

und seine Sammlung griechischer Handschriften," *Zentralblatt für Bibliothekswesen*, xv, 1898, p. 345–357, 393–420, 441–482, 537–566 (also issued as a separate by Harrassowitz in 1898; reviewed by Karl Krumbacher in the *Byzantinische Zeitschrift*, viii, 1899, p. 560–561). See also Gardthausen, *Katalog der griechischen Handschriften der Universitäts-Bibliothek zu Leipzig.*

58. Klenz, *op. cit.*, p. 53.

59. Ada Sara Adler, *D. G. Moldenhawer og hans Haandskriftsamling.* Copenhagen: J. L. Lybecker, 1917. (Copenhagen thesis.)

60. Review of Adler's thesis in *Deutsche Literaturzeitung*, xxxix, 1918, p. 790–791.

61. Louis Karl, "Incunables et livres précieux volés à la Bibliothèque de l'Université à Graz," *Revue des Bibliothèques*, xl, 1930, p. 191–194. See also "Thefts of Rare Books," *Libraries*, xxxvi, 1931, p. 137–138.

62. Item in the column "Vermischte Notizen," *Zentralblatt für Bibliothekswesen*, ii, 1885, p. 294.

63. Camille Pittolet, "À propos de récents vols de livres en Espagne avec quelques souvenirs sur la bibliothèque Colombine," *Revue des Bibliothèques*, xl, 1930, p. 40–58, and "Vols à la 'Biblioteca Nacional' de Madrid," *ibid.*, p. 203–204.

64. G. C. Kapur, "The Problem of Book Losses in Libraries," *Modern Librarian*, Lahore, viii, no. 1, Oct.-Dec., 1931, p. 18.

65. A. S. W. Rosenbach, *The Unpublishable Memoirs.* London: John Castle, 1924.

66. Cim, *op. cit.*, p. 25–26.

67. *ibid.*, p. 55–58.

68. *The Origin of Printing in Europe.* Chicago: University of Chicago Press, 1940. p. 19. Butler refers only to the Middle Ages here, but it might not be amiss to extend to, or perhaps even through, the nineteenth century the period when the Church was a refuge for learned men of all varieties.

69. Kapur, *op. cit.*, p. 18; Sander, *op. cit.*, p. 160.

70. Gardthausen, *Handbuch der wissenschaftlichen Bibliothekskunde.* Leipzig: Quelle & Meyer, 1920, i, p. 177; Cim, *op. cit.*, p. 66–80; J. C. F. Hoefer, *Nouvelle biographie universelle.* Paris: Firmin Didot frères, 1852–1866, iii, p. 900; Jean-Barthélemy Hauréau, *Singularités historiques et littéraires.* Paris: Michel Levy frères, 1861. p. 286–324.

71. Published in 1798 in The Hague as *Monuments authentiques de la religion grecque.*

72. H. Omont, "Les vols d'Aymon à la Bibliothèque du Roi et le Baron de Stosch," *Revue des Bibliothèques*, i, 1891. p. 468–469. Stosch's collection was later acquired for the Vatican by Cardinal Passionei *(infra)*.

73. Klenz, *op. cit.*, p. 52: Harald Wieselgren, *Drottning Kristinas bibliotek och bibliotekarier före hennes bosättning i Rom*. Stockholm: Kungliga boktryckeriet, P. A. Norstedt & söner, 1901. K. *Vitterhets, historie och antiqvitets akademiens handlingar* n.f., xiii, 2; Anders Grape and Otto von Friesen, *Om Codex Argenteus. dess tid, hem och öden*. Uppsala: Svenska litteratursällskapet, 1928; *Svenska litteratursällskapets skrifter*, xxvii. p. 174–176.

74. Even this was not the end of the tribulations of Ulfilas' famous book, for during the nineteenth century someone stole ten leaves from the Gospel of St. Mark; but fortunately they were later recovered. Grape and von Friesen, *op. cit.*, p. 174–176.

75. There is an introductory bibliography on Passionei in Bohatta's article in the *Lexikon des gesamten Buchwesens*, ii, p. 623. See also Sander, *op. cit.*, p. 160.

76. Karl Justi, *Winckelmann; sein Leben, seine Werke und seine Zeitgenossen*. Leipzig: F. C. W. Vogel, 1866–1872. ii, p. i, 97; and Cim, *op. cit.*, p. 12–15.

77. Lalanne, *op. cit.*, p. 189–190.

78. Cim, *op. cit.*, p. 20–21.

79. Bohatta lists the more important references on Chavin de Malan in the *Lexikon des gesamten Buchwesens*, i, p. 339. Particularly important are Maillard, *op. cit.*, p. 110–115, and Bogeng, *Streifzüge eines Bücherfreundes*, i, p. 177.

80. Maillard, *op. cit.*, p. 114.

81. Cim, *op. cit.*, p. 125–127.

82. Klenz, *op. cit.*, p. 53.

83. Cited in A. R. Spofford, *A Book for All Readers*. New York: C. P. Putnam's Sons, 1900. p. 138–139.

84. *ibid.*

85. M. A. Bullard, "Book Thieves," *Library Journal*, x, 1885. p. 380.

86. "Books Stolen from Public Libraries," *Library Journal*, xxix, 1904. p. 76–77.

87. For bibliography see Bohatta's article in *Lexikon des gesamten Buchwesens*, iii, p. 522, and Bogeng, *Die grossen Bibliophilen*, iii, p. 248. See also Sander, *op. cit.*, p. 155–158. Andrew Lang, *op. cit.*, p. 54–56, gives an account of Don Vincente in his inimitable style; and Cim's version, *op. cit.*, p. 28–50, is also well worth reading. Of course, no one interested in Don Vincente will fail to read Flaubert's masterful tale entitled "Bibliomanie," which was inspired by the Spanish priest.

88. For bibliography see Bohatta's article in the *Lexikon des gesamten Buchwesens*, iii, p. 401, and Bogeng, *Die grossen Bibliophilen*. See also Sander, *op. cit.*, p. 158–159.

89. Leipzig: Reclam, 1914; *Universalbibliothek*, no. 5816.

90. Klenz, *op. cit.*, p. 52. See also Karl Halm, "Friedrich Linden-brog," in Rochus Freiherr von Liliencron, ed., *Allgemeine deutsche Biographie*. Leipzig: Duncker und Humblot, 1875–1912. XVIII, p. 692–693. This article (which includes a short bibliography) makes no reference to the alleged theft. However, the unsigned article on Heinrich Lindenbrog, *ibid.*, p. 693, attributes the theft to him but goes on to say that he always denied it.

91. Cim, *op. cit.*, p. 15–18.

92. Gardthausen, *Handbuch der wissenschaftlichen Bibliothek-skunde*, I, p. 178; J. J. Tikkanen, *Die Psalterillustration in Mittel-alter; Band I, Die Psalterillustration in der Kunstgeschichte; Heft 1, Byzantinische Psalterillustration, mönchisch-theologische Redak-tion*. Helsingfors: Druekerei der Finnischen Litteratur-Gesellschaft, 1895, reviewed by J. Strzygowski in the *Byzantinische Zeitschrift*, VI, 1897, p. 422–426.

93. Sava Chalindaros, "Brief über die Begebenheiten auf dem Athos im letzten Jahrzehut," *Byzantinische Zeitschrift*, IX, 1900, p. 322–326.

94. Catalogued in Wilhelm Studemund, Leopold Cohn, and Karl de Boor, *Verzeichniss der griechischen Handschriften der Köni-glichen Bibliothek zu Berlin*. Berlin: A. Ascher, 1890–1897; *Die Handschriften-Verzeichnisse der Königlichen Bibliothek zu Berlin*, XI. See introduction to second part (on an unnumbered leaf) by Karl de Boor.

95. Maillard, *op. cit.*, p. 120–121.

96. Federico Patetta, "Come il manoscritto Udinese della così detta 'Lex Romana Raetica Curiensis' e un prezioso codice Ses-soriano saino emigrati dall' Italia," *Atti della R. Accademia delle Scienze di Torino*, XLVI, 1910–9111, p. 497–511; R. Helssig, "Der Erwerb des Codex Utinensis und einer anderen Julianhandscrift durch Gustav Hänel," *Zentralblatt für Bibliothekswesen*, XXIX, 1912, p. 97–116; Patetta, "L'esodo dall' Italia del Codex Utinensis e la sua rivendicabilità," *Atti della R. Accademia delle Scienze di Torino*, XLVIII, 1911–1912, p. 738–762; Helssig, "Nochmals der Erwerb des Codex Utinensis durch Gustav Hänel," *Zentralblatt für Bibliothekswesen*, XXIX, 1912, p. 510–519.

97. "Biblio-kleptomania and How to Check It," *Library World*, XVIII, 1906, p. 207–208.

98. *op. cit.*, p. 42–44.

99. I am indebted to Joshua Bloch, Chief of the Jewish Division of The New York Public Library for this story.

100. But sometimes, as in the case of Urdich, a concatenation of circumstances may make a biblioclast of the biblioklept. Very re-cently there was a possible case of where one common book thief destroyed far more volumes than he could ever have preserved.

There is an ugly and fantastic rumor to the effect that a certain South American library which recently was razed by fire was deliberately destroyed by one of the librarians who had stolen so many rarities from it that he felt compelled to burn the remainder in order to cover his tracks.

101. A book thief who combined all the worst features of his clan was a patron of the Astor Library who tore sixty pages from the *Revue de Paris,* converted them unlawfully to his own use, and to cap the climax committed plagiarism by translating the criminally abstracted leaves and selling the translation to *Appleton's Journal* as an original article. See Spofford, *op. cit.,* p. 137.

102. "Paris Bibliothèque de l'École des Beaux Arts," *Library Journal,* xxxii, 1907, p. 239.

103. Uncaptioned anonymous note in *Zentralblatt für Bibliothekswesen,* xviii, 1901, p. 278.

104. L. Stainier, "Le Contrôle de la restitution des ouvrages donnés en lecture à la Bibliothèque Royale de Belgique," *Revue des bibliothèques et archives de Belgique,* ii, 1904, p. 253–263.

105. Gaillard, *op. cit.,* p. 8–9; Pittolet, *op. cit.,* p. 44–55; Henry Harrisse, *Grandeur et décadence de la Colombine.* Paris: Les Marchands de Nouveautés, 1885, 2nd ed.; "Extrait de la *Revue Critique,* n° du 18 mai 1885." Colombiana as well as the contents of Fernando Columbus' library seem to have a special attraction for thieves. The New York Public Library copy of the pictorial (1493) edition of the Latin translation of the Columbus letter enjoys the reputation of being unique, thanks to a thief who removed the only other known copy from the Brera Library in Milan early in the nineteenth century. See Wilberforce Eames, ed., *The Letter of Columbus on the Discovery of America.* New York: The Lenox Library, 1892. p. vi, note 2.

106. O. Hartwig, "Zur Geschichte der Colombina in Sevilla," *Zentralblatt für Bibliothekswesen,* ii, 1885, p. 330–331.

107. "Book Thieves' Vade Mecum," *Bulletin of the Massachusetts Library Club,* xxiii, 1933, p. 3–6.

108. "Stealing a Whole Library," *loc. cit.*

109. "Recent Arrest of Cincinnati Bookseller," *Publishers' Weekly,* cxxx, 1936, p. 1630.

110. "Stolen Books," *Publishers' Weekly,* cxxxi, 1937, p. 1406.

111. "Rare Book Thief Caught," *Publishers' Weekly,* cxix, 1931, p. 2791–2792.

112. "Notorious Book Thief," *Library Journal,* lxi, 1936, p. 859–860.

113. "Book Thief Caught," *Publishers' Weekly,* cxxxi, 1937, p. 2179.

114. Federal law also forbids receiving and pledging of stolen

property transported in interstate commerce and in the case of pledging, the property need not be valued at more than $500.
115. However, this was not William John Kwiatowski's first brush with Uncle Sam. In 1936 he had been arrested and sentenced for a violation of the postal laws in connection with an attempt to sell a stolen volume by use of the United States mails. He was given another sentence in 1936 for violation of the copyright laws committed when he attempted to sell as his own a magazine article plagiarized from a copyrighted publication.
116. For a full account of this case by the Assistant United States Attorney who prosecuted it, see Robert M. Hitchcock, "Case of a Missing Shakespeare," *Esquire*, xvi, December, 1941, p. 93.
117. Edward Walter Kwiatowski's sentence was suspended, and he was placed on probation for two years.
118. *op. cit.*, p. 130–136.
119. "Book Thieves: An Incident and Some Suggestions," *Library Journal*, xxix, 1904, p. 308–309.
120. Robert Kendall Shaw, "The Perfect Bibliomaniac," *Library Journal*, lvii, 1932, p. 1062–1063. Included in the haul were three volumes of the *New Century Dictionary*, Holbrook Jackson on bibliomania, Blades' *Enemies of Books*, and *Condemned to Devil's Island*.
121. Haakon Fiskaa, "Store boktyverier fra universitetsbiblioteket i Aberdeen," *Bog og bibliotek*, iii, 1936, p. 244.
122. *loc. cit.*
123. *loc. cit.* As the result of an epidemic of theft in the libraries of wartime Britain, there have been some recent valuable contributions by English public library authorities. Especially important is Robert Lewis Wright Collison's "Crime in Libraries," *Library World*, xliv, 1941, p. 133–135, a survey of library protective law in the United Kingdom and a tabulation of recorded thefts showing the nature of the losses in English public libraries. See also Wright's "Universal Practice," *Library World*, lxiv, 1941, p. 65–66, and "Stop Thief!," *Librarian and Book World*, xxxi, 1941, p. 74.
124. "Conscience Week," *Library Journal*, lxvi, 1941, p. 361. Many strays also return in the course of book drives such as the Victory Book Campaign sponsored by American librarians early in the war. See Jesse Cunningham, "Victory Books A.W.O.L.," *Library Journal*, lxvii, 1942, p. 375.
125. Ruth Anne Bean, "Theft and Mutilation of Books, Magazines and Newspapers," *Library Occurent*, Indiana State Library, xii, January-March, 1936, p. 12–15. A refreshing contrast to this pusillanimity was the attitude of S. Green, "Capture of a Notorious Book Thief," *Library Journal*, 1, 1880, p. 48–49.

126. See Ralph Munn, "The Problems of Theft and Mutilation," *Library Journal*, LX, 1935, p. 589–592. *Horrible dictu*, Munn reports that our schools are actually teaching innocent children to be Grangerizers under a so-called "project method"!

127. *op. cit.*, p. 101.

128. *ibid.*, p. 58–59.

129. *ibid.*, p. 24–25, 107–116.

130. There is a brief survey and bibliography by Edgar Breitenbach in his article "Stockholm" in the *Lexikon des gesamten Buchwesens*, III, p. 341.

131. Margaret Burton, *Famous Libraries of the World*. London: Grafton, 1937; *The World's Great Libraries*, II, p. 316.

132. Arundel Esdaile, *National Libraries of the World: Their History, Administration, and Public Services*. London: Grafton, 1934; *The World's Great Libraries*, I, p. 147–148.

133. "Virginia's Stolen Manuscripts," *Library Journal*, XXXVII, 1912, p. 391.

A Cursory Survey of Maledictions

DON'T BE SURPRISED when the members of the staff of The New York Public Library break out with leprosy, acquire hideous physical deformities, and are taken away for a sojourn in the penitentiary. They will be in good company in their misfortunes. Plagues will probably be rampant in the British Museum; librarians of the Bibliothèque Nationale will be languishing in the nether regions with Judas the Traitor; and the custodians of the Oesterreichische Nationalbibliothek will be hanging from the highest gallows in Vienna. Most libraries harbor books that once were stolen. The volumes they now guard so zealously were, in many instances, once the property of other libraries; and in not a few of them may be found gravely composed curses condemning thieves to all manner of physical and spiritual torment. Throughout the Middle Ages and the first two or three centuries of modern times the book curse was one of the principal devices for the protection of library books from potential biblioklepts.

The administrative problems of the medieval library—and "medieval" in the bibliothecal sense extends up to the present day in not a few cases—consisted largely in acquiring and possessing, with considerably less emphasis on use. Chaining,[1] strict regulations on the loan privilege,[2] large deposits demanded as a guarantee of a book's return,[3] and, perhaps most frequently of all, miniatory statements directed at potential thieves were the commonly used administrative devices to protect the literary property of the medieval library. Medieval man was so deeply concerned with the next world that he thought he could best protect his books in this vale of tears by the mere threat of damnation there.

But in this as in so much else, medieval man was not original. The book curse was known to the Director of Ashur-bani-pal's library in ancient Assyria, and well-nigh every volume of any importance in that collection had the following inscription:

> The palace of Ashur-bani-pal, king of hosts, king of Assyria, who putteth his trust in the gods Ashur and Bêlit, on whom Nabû and Tashmetu have bestowed ears which hear and eyes which see. I have transcribed upon tablets the noble products of the work of the scribe which none of the kings who had gone before me had learned, together with the wisdom of Nabû in so far as it existeth [in writing]. I have arranged them in classes, I have revised them and I have placed them in my palace, that I, even I, the ruler who knoweth the light of Ashur, the king of the gods, may read them. Whosoever shall carry off this tablet, or shall inscribe his name on it, side by side with mine own, may Ashur and Bêlit overthrow him in wrath and anger, and may they destroy his name and posterity in the land.[4]

When Christian congregations began to collect books in the third century, the fathers began to give serious consideration to the problem of preserving the integrity of the texts over which they were the custodians. Rufinus Tyrannius, translating Origen's *De Principiis*, threatened those who would tamper with his text with damnation in "the place where there is wailing and gnashing of teeth and where the fire never goes out."[5] When the seventy-two learned Jews at the court of Ptolemy Philadelphus undertook the Greek translation of the Old Testament, later known as the Septuagint to commemorate this spurious tradition, the king is alleged to have placed a curse on all who would make so bold as to attempt to change the text.[6] However, this malediction seems to have had little effect, for Origen and many others after him attempted to improve on the text of the Alexandrian translators.

But the church was interested almost as much in the protection of its physical property as in maintaining the texts inviolate. It is not surprising, therefore, that the early fathers recognized in the curse against those who would alter texts a potentially effective device which could also be used against possible biblioklepts. The oriental congregations quickly took up the tradition of the curse and revised it to apply to the book itself. In a seventh-or eighth-century Syriac manuscript from the famous convent of Deyr-es-Suriani or St. Mary Deipara in the Nitrian Desert (Wady Nâtron) there is an anathema reading: "May the name of the individual who destroys this memorandum [that the book was bought for the monastery] be deleted from the Book of Life."[7] William Wright comments in his preface to the third and last part of his catalog:

> The finished volume was now deposited in the library for which it was intended. The librarian made an entry on one of the fly-leaves of the name of the donor and the date of the gift, in most cases adding an anathema against any one who should injure, mutilate, or steal it. Books were, however, lent for the purposes of copying, collation or study, and the rules of the library of S. Mary Deipara were so liberal as to allow six months for these purposes.[8]

Eastern Europe knew the book curse well. In the famed book collections of Mount Athos, there were manuscript notations of ownership which also carried threats against book thieves with the curse of the twelve apostles and all the monks.[9] Wattenbach cites. a Greek example from the fifteenth century, showing characteristic linguistic deficiencies of the period:

Εἴτιϛ το ἠοτϲρϲισι να εἶνυι ἀφορισμένοϛ παρὰ τηϛ ἁγίαϛ τριάδοϛ χαὶ τὸ αἰωνίω ἀναθέματι.[10]

In 1608 Abbas the Great, shah of Persia, founded a library at Ardebil in honor of his ancestor Sefi (died 334); and when Count Paul von Suchtelen sent the collection to St. Petersburg after Ardebil fell to the Russians in 1829, it was found that on the first page of every book Abbas invoked on the thief the worst of all fates that could befall a Shiite, that the blood of Imam Husaim, Mohamet's angel who fell at Kerbela, be on his hands.[11]

The earliest book curses used in the West seem to be imprecations of the donors of books who sought to protect the religious establishments endowed by their generosity. Thus when Theodetrud made a gift to Saint-Denis in 627 there was a provision in the manuscript for disease, damnation, and ruin to be visited upon the thief.[12] On the other hand, a picturesque malediction in a ninth-century manuscript of Cassiodorus' *Historia tripartita*, at one time in Monte Cassino, reads in part (on F. 1ᵃ): "Siquis *nobis* hunc librum quolibet modo malo ingenio tollere temptaverit aut voluerit, sit *anathema* Maranatha."[13] There can be little doubt but that this inscription was inserted by the monastic administration rather than by a donor. As the monasteries began to expand, the inmates began to be ever more zealous in the protection of their property, and the type of curse found in Monte Cassino began to be duplicated all over western Europe. While the practice was not the result of a directive from the Papal See, it was probably within the right of every abbot to place an anathema on a book thief. Indeed, many monastic librarians sought to protect their property not by curses but by gentle pleas. For example, Reginbert of Reichenau provided books he copied with a rhymed appeal to the better nature of would-be thieves; but these appeals were of no avail when Count Libri caught sight of these manuscripts some hundreds of years later.[14]

Libri had absolutely no respect for the laboriously composed curses of medieval librarians. Léopold Delisle found a curious example of Libri's handicraft in a manuscript of extracts from the works of St. Gregory, at one time manuscript no. 51 of the Orléans, France, Public Library. Originally the property of the Abbey of Fleuri-sur-Loire, Libri altered the statement of ownership to make it appear as if the manuscript came from a Florentine abbey but at the same time he left unchanged the curse damning him to perpetual torment in the evil company of Annas, Caiaphas, Pilate, and Judas.[15]

Some monasteries interpreted the right to curse book thieves in an even broader sense and bound their inmates by strict regulations against lending. Even an innocent circulation librarian might conceivably run afoul of an anathema simply because he lent his book. However, the church took official cognizance of this situation, and in 1212 a council met in Paris and issued the following decree:

> We forbid those who belong to a religious order to formulate any vow against lending their books to those who are in need of them, seeing that to lend is enumerated among the principal works of mercy.
>
> After careful consideration, let some books be kept in the house for the use of brethren, others, according to the decision of the abbot, be lent to those who are in need of them, the rights of the house being safeguarded.
>
> From the present date, no book is to be retained under pain of incurring a curse [for its alienation], and we declare all such curses to be of no effect.[16]

How little attention was paid to this directive is obvious enough from the history of librarianship, for only in our own century have the custodians of books learned that lending is among the principal works of mercy. And while a few timid souls may have been frightened into discarding the book curse as an administrative device, it continued to thrive luxuriantly in most quarters. Princes of the church did not hesitate to invoke the highest authority for the protection of bibliothecal treasures, and we even find St. Peter watching over the Biblioteca Apostolica Vaticana as he "*sacrorum* librorum thesaurum in Romana ecclesia perpetuo asservari jubet."[17]

No less severe a fate than excommunication was threatened in many a book curse, and often as not the threat was specifically made on papal authority. When Charles v, at the request of Bishop Pierre de Villars of Troyes, gave some relics and books to the Dominicans of that city, the gift was accompanied by a special bull of Gregory xi, issued under the date of 26 February 1371, forbidding their alienation on the pain of excommunication.[18] Nevertheless, in spite of this drastic step, the books were dispersed in the sixteenth century during the administration of an ignorant prior. Some have found a final resting place in the Bibliothèque Nationale, others in the Troyes Public Library.

Gregory XI was not the only pope who shook the big stick of excommunication at potential biblioklepts. From inscriptions on certain volumes of the Biblioteca Apostolica Vaticana the following lines have been quoted:

> Si quis secus fecerit, libros partemve aliquam abstulerit, extraxerit, clepserit, rapseritque, carpserit, corruperit dolo malo, ille a fidelium communione ejectus, maledictus anathematis vinculo colligatus esto. A quoquam praeterquam Romano Pontifice ne absolvitur.[19]

In the early eighteenth century there appeared on the book plate of the Benedictine monastery of St. Peter at Salzburg a threat of excommunication quoted from a bull of Clement XI.[20] Gottfried and Aegidius Gelen, two of the most distinguished priests in Cologne in the seventeenth century, composed their own "Tenor excommunicationis latae sententiae a raptoribus et detentoribus librorum Bibliotecae Geleniae ipso facto incurrendae . . ." and inscribed it on a book-plate which has survived.[21]

In many instances no specific papal authority was invoked, and the individual donor or monastic administrator assumed the authority for pronouncing anathema. Blanche of Castille, one of the more distinguished lady bibliophiles of the Middle Ages, presented a Bible to the Abbey of St. Victor a little before 1250 and inscribed the following note therein:

> Iste liber est Sancti Victoris Parisiensis. Quicumque eum furatus fuerit vel celaverit vel titulum istum deleverit, anathema sit. Hanc bibliothecam dedit ecclesie Sancti Victoris Parisiensis Blancha illustria regina Francie, mater regis Ludowici.[22]

In other cases even higher authority than the papal was invoked. The Council of Nicea, whose principal business is generally recorded as the suppression of Arianism, was perverted to an institute on library management by a fourteenth-century Greek monk. At the end of an exegetical work on the Psalms, this pious fellow called upon the 318 Nicene fathers to punish anyone who should steal the fruit of his labors; and to strengthen his case, he added the curse of the Holy Trinity, the Mother of God, John the Baptist, and all the saints. To make absolutely certain of the efficacy of his malediction, he expressed the hope at the end that the thief would suffer the fate of Sodom and Gomorrha and would hang from the noose of Judas Iscariot.[23]

The dread fate of Judas Iscariot made a terrifying impression on the medieval world.[24] It was worse to have the guilt of having betrayed the Lord to weigh on one's eternal conscience than to worry about the relatively simple matter of excommunication. That Judas, the arch villain, hung himself may well have some connection with the threat of the gallows, the *gibet*, the *Galgen* that will reappear constantly in later miniatory inscriptions. Archer Taylor of the Berkeley branch of the University of California has written exhaustively on "The Judas Curse" in *The American Journal of Philology*.[25] Not only in the West but also in the Levant, Judas was considered the greatest of all sinners, and Greek and Syrian monasteries as well as English and German ones threatened book thieves with his fate. For example, in the Public Library of Leningrad, U.S.S.R., there is an Arabic inscription on the fly-leaf of a Syriac manuscript reading—

> This blessed book belongs to the church of the monastery of Sinai, and whosoever takes it away or tears a leaf from it, may the Virgin be a foe to him, and may his fate be one with the fate of Judas Iscariot.[26]

Taylor found a similar curse in a fourteenth-century Arabic manuscript of New Testament apocrypha which belonged to the convent of Deyr-es-Suriani, in a Greek version in a twelfth-century manuscript of Symeon Metaphrastes, and in many other sources, both oriental and occidental. While the Greek curses are likely as not to toss in the authority of the 318

Nicene fathers, the general pattern is similar to the commonly occurring one in the West, "Qui te furetur, cum Juda dampnificetur."
It is hardly surprising that among the first laymen to seize upon the book curse as a protective device were attorneys. In the rhymed prologue to the *Sachsenspiegel*, written around 1240, Eike von Repgow wrote:

> Groôz angest gêt mich an;
> ich vorchte daz manich man
> Diz bûch wille mêren,
> unde beginne recht virkêrren,
> Unde zì des ane mich.
> sô weiz mich Got unschuldich,
> Den dâ nieman kan betrûgen,
> Der wizze ouch daz sie liegen,
> Des ne kan ich nicht bewaren.
> alle die unrechte varen,
> Unde werven an disseme bûche,
> den send ich disse vlûche,
> Unde de valsch hîr zû scriben
> diu miselsucht muz in beclîben.[27]

Following closely on the heels of the priest and the jurist, the schoolboy, the collector, the government clerk, indeed, almost every person who dealt with books in the Middle Ages, began to use the book curse. Rabbis and other learned Jews did not hesitate to use this characteristic device of Christians and one might well suspect that a competent student of Jewish palaeography could turn up many more in addition to those recorded by Steinschneider,[28] Leiningen-Westerburg,[29] Crüwell,[30] and Meisner.[31]

Medieval man took the book curse quite seriously in many instances. He was not a person to use in vain the names of sacred persons, the 318 Nicene fathers, or even Judas Iscariot or Pilate; and leprosy and *miselsucht* were words that quite properly inspired fear in the hearts of men who lived in pre-Public Health Service days. Crüwell even managed to dig up a curious late seventeenth-century inscription which sought to

frighten the biblioklept not with the fear of eternal damnation
but rather with fear of his health: "Dies Bethbichl ist in Hendt
eins Pestkrankh gewest. Man mag es sohin nicht weitter
geben."[32] There is abundant evidence that medieval readers
respected the book curse as though it were a supernatural
directive. C. F. W. Jacobs and F. A. Ukert found a striking
example of the effect of a book curse in a relatively late period. In an English manuscript dating from the Anglo-Saxon
period there is the following curse: "Liber S. Mariae de Ponte
Roberti; qui eum abstulerit vel quamlibet eius partem absci-
deret, sit anathema Maranatha. Amen." When Bishop John
Grandison of Exeter acquired this manuscript in the four-
teenth century, he made sure of the purity of his record by
adding the following note: "Ego Johannes Exon Episcopus,
nescio ubi est domus praedicta, nec hunc librum abstulit, sed
modo legitimo adquissivi."[33]

Some of the charecteristic miniatory inscriptions in medieval
books were collected by Jakob Wichner in his study of
Admont,[34] a Styrian monastery founded in the eleventh century. Hanging and beating are the most common threats, and
one might well suspect that in many parts of Europe such
threats were carried out quite literally against thieves who had
had the ill luck to be caught. A few examples will reveal the
type of curse that might be found in Admont as well as in
other medieval libraries:

> Qui me furetur, me reddat vel suspendatur.
> Qui me furetur, baculo bene percutietur.
>
> Qui fraudauerit hunc anathemate percutia⎤
> Atque dei genitricis eum vindicta sequa ⎦ tur.
>
> Lauda scriptorem, donec videas meliorem.
> Non uideat Christum, qui librum substrahit istum.

The group collected by Josef Klapper[35] of Breslau is also
typical of the verbal defenses of the medieval librarian:

> Si quis furatus fuerit librum istum aut invenit et non
> reddiderit fratri Johanni Carnificis, anathema sit.

Explicit liber omeliarum pars secunda sancte Marie uirginis
in Zagano. Quem qui fraudauerit vel sponte uniolaverit,
anathema sit. Amen.

Sorte supernorum scriptor libri pociatur,
Morte malignorum raptor libri moriatur.

Qui te furetur, tribus lignis associetur.

Qui rapit hunc librum, demon frangat sibi collum.

The repeated and constant use of the book curse did no good
to the efficacy of the custom, for unquestionably there were
many cases of unpunished theft. Furthermore, the very nature
of the book curse, an exaggerated threat which, in most instances, was far too severe punishment for an ordinary book
theft, was another weakening element. It is only too well
known that in many cases learned renaissance gentlemen
were compelled to resort to drastic measures in order to retrieve valuable manuscripts from their clerical custodians; and
there has been hardly a complaint in later generations that
any disservice was done to scholarship by this thievery to
achieve a high-minded purpose. In other instances, where
every single book in a library was annotated with a curse, as
in the case of the collection of Charles v given to the Dominicans at Troyes, no very serious attention was likely to be paid
to mere formula.[36] Finally, the pseudo-learned character of
the book curse made it an ideal vehicle for schoolboys and
pranksters who would satirize a traditional device of the
medieval copyist.

The weakness of the book curse in the late Middle Ages is
only too well illustrated by the unwillingness of owners of
books to rely solely upon it as a protection against delinquent
borrowers. The faculty of medicine at Paris, a realistic group
of scholarly gentlemen, was unwilling in 1471 to take the royal
word of Louis xi or even to trust the efficacy of a curse when
he borrowed the works of the Arabian physician Rhasis. He
was forced to deposit a large quantity of valuable plate, and
he was also compelled to procure a nobleman to join him in
a deed to secure the return of the book.[37]

But even as early as the tenth century the significance of

the book curse had been questioned. The whimsical becomes the order of the day from the eleventh century on. Consider, for example, the cleverly composed couplet found in an eleventh-century manuscript:

Sor	supern	scrip	li	poti	
te	orum	tor	bri		atur.[38]
Mor	superb	rap	li	mori	

The possible fates of the book thief become more and more picturesque. With an imaginative command of words worthy of a nineteenth-century Texan or Kentuckian, one abbot wished that the thief would be punished with blows, the plague, leprosy, and a hunchback. Not only are obscure references made to Maranatha, but Dathan and Abiram are excavated from biblical oblivion. Thus in the church at Hermannstadt there was a missal compiled in 1394 by Herr Michael, parson at Klein Scheuern, and copied by one Theoderich, in which the following threat is made: "Qui nituntur eum auferre de fraternitate, descendant in infernum viventus cum Dathan et Abyron."[39]

The rhymed curse, of which several have already been cited, becomes more and more common as copyists began to look for humorous effects. In other cases, where the copyist felt compelled to say that book theft was wicked, without devising any effective preventive measure, he threw in a highly abbreviated form of the curse, such as, for example, the following appendage to the dedication of a manuscript by Archbishop Remigius of Lyons: "Sit utenti gratia, largitori venia *fraudanti anathema.*"[10]

But the boldest step towards making the curse a humorous formalism came when copyists began using the vernacula. Barely two centuries after Eike von Repgow's solemn warning in the *Sachsenspiegel* the following verse appeared in a German book:

> Wer das puch stehl, desselben chel
> Muzze sich ertoben
> Hoch an eim Galgen oben.[41]

Another German condemnation of the book thief to the gallows cannot be too far removed in point of time:

> Dass buch ist mir lib,
> wer mirss sthilt, der ist ein dip:
> ess sey ryter oder knecht,
> so ist her an den galgen gerecht.[42]

And surely one of the earliest is the one spotted in the Harleian Catalogue (no. 1251) by Wattenbach:

> Thy boke is one
> and Godes Kors ys anoder;
> They take the ton,
> God gefe them the toder.[43]

In sixteenth-century England there was a plethora of quaintly humorous miniatory inscriptions in contemporary books. In a book with a 1540 imprint appeared the following threat of the gallows:

> My Master's name above you se,
> Take heede therefore you steale not mee;
> For if you doe, without delay
> Your necke . . . for me shall pay.
> Looke doune below and you shal see
> The picture of the gallowstree;
> Take heede therefore of thys in time,
> Lest on this tree you highly clime.
> [Drawing of the gallows][44]

And another dated but a few years later appears in a Sarum manuscript captioned "Vigiliae mortuorum":

> Thomas Hyllbrond owe this book,
> Whosoever will yt tooke,
> Whoso stellyt shall be hangyd,
> By ayre, by water, or by lande.
> With a hempen bande.
> God is where he was.
> A° Vi. R. Edwardi vi.[45]

Under the date of 1623 the following entry occurs in the church register of Sowe, Warwickshire (which commences in 1538):

Who lets this book be lost,
Or doth embesell yt,
God's curse will to his cost,
Give him plagues in hell fytt.[46]

One hesitates to ascribe without further evidence any great antiquity to a threat found on a book-plate of a volume purchased in an antiquarian shop in 1920:

Who folds a leafe downe ye divel toaste browne,
Who makes marke or blotte ye divel roaste hot,
Who stealeth thisse boke ye divel shall cooke.[47]

Fifteenth-century France can also produce a vernacular curse on a book thief from a manuscript in the library of Jean d'Orléans, comte d'Angoulême. Jean was a captive in England for thirty-three years during the reign of Henry VI, and he seems to have beguiled the wearisome years with bibliophilic pursuits. M. Dupont-Ferrier has collected notices of 167 manuscripts in Jean's collections, and in one of them he found a miniatory inscription:

Qui che live emblera
À gibet de Paris pendu sera,
Et, si n'est pendu, il noiera,
Et, si ne noie, il ardera,
Et, si n'aert pitte fin fera.[48]

H. Rayment, commenting on this inscription in *Notes and Queries*, suggests that the last line should properly be read "et, si n'art, pire fin fera."[49]

The Latin inscriptions from the Renaissance on begin to assume a distinctly modern note. The acquisitive society so foreign to medieval teachings appears in those inscriptions which clearly indicate that there is an owner and that he has written his name in the book. Thus a fifteenth-century book belonging to the Society of Antiquaries contains these lines:

Reddatur domino a quocunque repertas;
Non opus est quaeras, aspice, nomen habes.[50]

The severity of the Middle Ages is gradually lost in later centuries. No respectable book thief could ever be disturbed by such pusillanimous doggerel at that which appears in the books of Andreas Hedio, a mid-seventeenth-century professor at the University of Königsberg (Krolewicz):

> Me sibi jure suum Dominus, propriumque paravit;
> Usum concessit sponte cuicumque [?] bono.
> Sed tu, si bonus es, Domino me reddito gratus,
> Si retinas, malus es, nec bonus usus erit.[51]

Rather appropriately, these verses appear on Hedio's bookplate, consisting of his coat of arms, the head and shoulders of an old graybeard in a fish-tailed nightcap.

A far cry from the stern decrees of excommunication is the heavily declamatory ex-libris of Wessobrunn, a Benedictine monastery in the diocese of Freysingen in Bavaria (U. S. Zone). Under an enthroned pontiff with a long pastoral staff there are two limping hexameters:

> Wessofanti proba sum possessio claustri.
> Heus! Domino me redde meo: sic jura reposcunt.[52]

Or, in another case, a malediction is mollified by words of gentleness, wisdom, and piety:

> *Laus Deo semper.*
>
> Registre appartenant
> a
> Hendricque Honne
> Marchand et Menusier [*sic*]
> a
> Veruier anno 1697.
> Quisquis in hunc librum furtivos fixerit ungues
> Ibit ad infernas non rediturus aguas.
>
> ————————
>
> Virtutem primam esse puta complacere linguam
> Proximas ille Deo est qui scit ratione facere.
>
> ————————
>
> Si specto siccis oculis tua vulnera, Christe,
> Sum cruce, sum clavis durior ipsi tuis.
>
> +
> I. H. S.[35]

Learned eighteenth-century legal researchers decided that the book curse was null and void in any court action,[54] but it survived in folk books as a fairly serious matter. In the *Rosarium philosophicum*, a treatise on alchemy, dire threats not unlike the medieval curse are made against unworthy apprentices who might make so bold as to betray a secret of the processes of transmutation.[55] Even in such a learned work as Gabriel Barri's *De antiquitate et situ Calabriae* eighteenth-century editors still carried the threat against those who would translate the work into Italian, expressly stating that any such translator would live but one year longer. Yet we still have a picturesque malediction from the seventeenth or eighteenth century in Low German, a language which lends itself well to a semi-humorous curse:

> Dyt bock hort Methken vam Holte;
> De dat vind, de do dat wedder,
> Edder de Düvel vorbrennt em dat ledder
> Hoet dy![56]

Sherlock Willis' bookplate, an unmistakable Chippendale dated 1756, does not go to the extreme of damning the forgetful borrower, but it does put him to shame by quoting from Psalm xxxvi: "The ungodly borroweth and payeth not again . . ." Charles Ferdinand Hommeau set aside the book curse and blunty told borrowers: "If you do not return the loan within fourteen days, or do not keep it carefully, on another occasion [when you ask to borrow it or some other book] I shall say I have not got it.[57]

One of the last modern cases of an apparently serious malediction is that which was attached to the collection of Henrik Rantzau (died 1599), the royal Danish Statthalter for the duchy of Slesvik-Holstein. On his "golden" books in the library of Castle Breitenburg near Itzehoe, Holstein, he laid the following "perpetuum decretum":

HENRICI RANZOVII PER-
petuum de biblioteca sua
DECRETUM

> Quae infrà scripta sunt, hunc in modum sancta
>   sunto, inviolateque observantur.
> Ranzovii, nec quisquam alius, hanc possidento,
>   Haeredes eam non dividunto,
>   Nemini libros, codices volumina, picturas,
>   Ex ea auferendi, extrahendi,
>   Alióve apportandi,
>   Nisi licentia possessoris,
>   Facultas esto.
> Si quis secus fecerit;
>   Libros, partemve aliquam abstulerit,
>   Extraxerit, clepserit, rapserit,
>   Concerpserit, corruperit,
>   Dolo malo:
>   Illicò maledictus
>   Perpetuò execrabilis,
>   Semper detestabilis
>   Esto, maneto.[58]

But despite these strong words, Rantzau's fine library was dispersed when Wallenstein took Breitenburg on 29 September 1627. Parts of the collection may be found in many of the more important libraries of central and northern Europe. Better evidence of the ineffectiveness of the book curse as a protective device could hardly have been brought to the attention of the collector.

The purely humorous book curse began to appear at the dawn of the Renaissance. Perhaps the most unmistakable example is the macaronic verse, an early English example of which runs:

> Hic liber est meus,
> Testis est Deus,
> Si quisquis furetur,
> Per collum pendetur,
> Like hic poor cretur.[59]

On an eighteenth-century book cover in the Germanisches National-Museum in Nuremberg there is one of the most frequently quoted macaronic verses and one of the cleverest:

> Hic liber est mein,
> Ideo nomen meum scripsi drein;
> Si vis hunc librum stehlen,
> Pendebis an der Kehlen;
> Tunc veniunt die Raben
> Et volunt tibi oculos ausgraben,
> Tunc clamabis: Ach, ach, ach!
> Ubique tibi recte geschach.[60]

Many macaronics secure heightened effect by threatening explicit physical injury to biblioklepts. The next two have appeared in many forms, but those given below are the most common:

> Hic meus est liber
> And that I will show;
> Si aliquis rapiat
> I'll give him a blow.[61]

> Si quisquis furetur
> This little libellum,
> Per Bacchum, per Jovem!
> I'll kill him, I'll fell him,
> In ventrem illius
> I'll stick my scalpellum,
> And teach him to steal
> My little libellum.[62]

Of the many attractive French macaronics the best known is

> Aspice Pierrot pendu,
> Quod librum n'a pas rendu.
> Pierrot pendu non fuisset
> Si librum reddidisset.[62]

A crude drawing of Pierrot dangling from the gallows usually precedes this inscription. A somewhat longer version was turned up by a contributor to *Notes and Queries:*

> Qui ce livre derobera,
> Pro suis criminibus,
> Sa tête au gibet postera

> cum aliis latronibus;
> Quelle honte ce sera
> Pro suis parentibus.
> Si hunc librum reddidisset,
> Pierrot pendu non fuisset.[64]

Another French antiquarian, one Beaujour (pseud.), excavated
the following:

> Si hunc librum, par aventure,
> Reperies sur ton chemin,
> Redde mihi la couverture
> Quae facta est de parchemin;
> Ad bibendum à ma santé
> La jour nommé la Trinité.[65]

The ultimate in the attempts to lend a spot of humor to the
lex bibliothecae may be observed in William Barnes' well-
known tetraglott epigram:

> Si l'uom che deruba un tomo,
> Trium literarum est homo,
> Celui qui dérobe trois tomes
> A man of three letters must become.[66]

By way of annotation it should be explained that the Romans
politely referred to a thief as a "man of three letters" (*f, u, r*).

By this time no one should consider as especially serious
a miniatory inscription hoping that the biblioklept die the
death, be cooked upon a gridiron, suffer from fevers and the
falling sickness, and finally be broken upon the wheel and
hung.[67] Always a likely vehicle for the clever rhymster, the
book curse afforded nineteenth-century bookish wits the opportunity for a field day. Old miniatory inscriptions were
brought out and refurbished for use on modern book-plates,
and new ones illustrating the wit of a collector or a schoolboy
augmented the imposing list gathered by serious scholars such
as Delisle and Wattenbach. Neo-Latin inscriptions with clever
modernistic references lend color to the use of this ancient
language as a book curse. Old and new curses and inscriptions

crowd the columns of *Notes and Queries* and the *Intermédiaire des Chercheurs et Curieux.*

A few examples of schoolboy doggerel reveal the depths to which the book curse had descended by the last century:

> Small is the wren,
> Black is the rook;
> Great is the sinner that steals this book.

> This is Thomas Jones's book—
> You may just within it look;
> But you'd better not do more,
> For the Devil's at the door,
> And will snatch at fingering hands:
> Look behind you—there he stands![68]

The hangman's noose and blows with stout fists and cudgels were threats regularly made by small boys who were early imbued with the possessive instincts:

> This book is one thing,
> Hemp is another;
> Steal not this one thing,
> For fear of the other.
>   Wnpbo Shed.
>   1802.[69]

> This book is one thing,
> My fist is another;
> Touch this one thing,
> You'll sure feel the other.[70]

> If you this precious volume bone,
> Jack Ketch will claim you for his own.[71]

The collector of this last gem also tells of the owner of a library who used to insert a small gibbet, cut from cardboard, with the borrower's name thereon, projecting from the vacant place on his shelf.

The threat of eternal damnation was still used, but few thieves would worry seriously about taking a book inscribed

> Steal not this book for fear of shame,
> For in it is the owner's name,
> And when you die the Lord will say,
> Where is that book you stole away?[72]

But even this inscription is not exclusively concerned with spiritual well being in every instance. One version, reported by John Murray in a follow-up note to go with the above runs

> Steal not this book, mine honest friend,
> For fear the gallows be thine end.
> Steal not this book for fear of shame, etc.[73]

A common neo-Latin threat of the gallows is

> This book belongs to ....
> Si quis furetur
> Per collum pendetur
> In hoc modo.
> [Sketch of the gallows with a body hanging therefrom.][74]

In at least one instance a specific gallows is designated as the *locus mortis:*

> Steal not this book, my Friend,
> Least [sic] Tyburn be thy end.[75]

But the gallows and the fist were not the only threats. In a copy of Bunyan's *Parson's Booke of Christian Exercise* (1615) the following was observed in a seventeenth-century hand:

> Valentine Lawrence owneth this booke
> & he that stealeth it shalbe hanged on a crooke.[76]

The twentieth century has not been totally barren of book curses, if we may define as such the couplet

> Do not steal this book of knowledge,
> Or you'll be sent to Sing-Sing College.[77]

A rather clever modern miniatory inscription in German has been found in a book which once belonged to Alwin Starke, private in the Fourth Company of the 194th Regiment, Imperial German Army, and body servant to Lieutenant Erich Freiherr von Hausen at Chemnitz in 1881:

Dieses Buch ist mein eigen,
Wer es anfasst, kriegt Ohrfeigen.
Wer es wegnimmt, der kriegt Keile,
Das sage ich jetzt alleweile.
Bei meinem Herrn hab' ich's gut gehabt,
Das danke ich ihm tausendmal,
Bei dem da bin gern gewesen,
Das thut man in dem Buche lesen.[78]

Few countries of Western Europe cannot show some samples of modern schoolboy doggerel threatening potential thieves. A small Dutch boy in Zevenaar wrote the following:

(N. N.) hoor dit boek.
Die het vindt geeft het weer
Voor een appel of en peer,
Die het niet doet
Staat die galg voor den voet
En zal zitten op een rad,
Met zeven pinnen in het gat,
En zal roepen: o Heer! o Heer!
Geef (N. N.) dit boek weer!

Or take the one from De Zaansteek:

Dit boekje is mij lief,
Die het steelt die is een dief,
Heer of Knecht
Hangen is 't recht.[79]

On the other hand, in America there seem to be relatively few miniatory book inscriptions which are not traceable to English models.[80]

A large proportion of fly-leaf inscriptions are directed more against borrowers than against thieves. One rather cute piece from a high school textbook is

If thou art borrowed by a friend,
Right welcome shall he be,
To read, to study, not to lend,
But to return to me.

Not that imparted knowledge doth
Diminish learning's store,

> But books, I find, if often lent
> Return to me no more.[81]

A similar and equally innocuous inscription runs

> If this I lent to any one,
>   Pray keep it not too long;
> Keepe cleane and fair and send with care
> To whom it doth belong.[82]

Many a more explicit admonition to borrowers may be found in medieval and renaissance manuscripts. For example, in an early fifteenth-century manuscript cited by Klapper we find: "Et sic est finis. Quis invenit, Johanno Wardenbrugo reddere debit."[83] And in France there have also been collectors who have contented themselves with simply telling the dilatory borrower that he was a naughty fellow, e.g., "Honny soit qui ne me rend pas."[84]

The decline and fall of the book curse is one of the curiosities of the history of the book. It lasted much longer than might normally have been expected, largely due to the fact that it is so obviously a quaint medievalism. By the time of the Reformation the book curse was no more effective, as far as the minds of men were concerned, than the pious request of the publishers of the Tauchnitz editions: "Purchasers are earnestly requested not to introduce these volumes into England." Likewise, it was sheer cuteness, nothing more, of a modern collector to compose such a verse as

> Vor allem gib zurück das Buch,
> Ansonsten fällt auf dich mein Fluch . . .[85]

The church also began to soft-pedal the book curse, although its elimination was an extremely slow process, not being realized until long after the directive of the Council of Paris issued in 1212.[86] When the church saw herself despoiled of her treasures of manuscripts and printed books during the French Revolution and the nineteenth century, the clergy could hardly put much trust in the book curse.

Today Bills of Rights protect physical property against unlawful seizure, and finely elaborated copyright laws protect intellectual property. But while the Federal Copyright Office is doubtless more effective than a half-serious threat, we must nevertheless view the book curse as being among the first bits of evidence of the acquisitive instinct in the intellectual fields. However, fewer and fewer readers took the book curse seriously, and several centuries ago it degenerated into one of the most widely cultivated vehicles of bibliographical humor. Closely related to other varieties of miniatory fly-leaf inscriptions and admonitions to delinquent borrowers, the book curse was fused with these genres by the humorists. A clever warning on a modern bookplate may as frequently as not contain vestigial remnants of the ancient practice of the book curse; but the inspiration is a modern one, and the composition is likely to be born of the collector's own imagination. At all events, don't put your exclusive trust in the old-fashioned malediction as the sole protection of your books.

Notes . . .

1. The literature on chained libraries is rather extensive, but see especially Burnett Hillman Streeter, *The Chained Library* (London: Macmillan, 1931).
2. Discussions of this aspect of medieval library administration may be found in James Westfall Thompson, *The Medieval Library* (Chicago: University of Chicago Press, 1939); John Willis Clark, *The Care of Books: an Essay on the Development of Libraries and Their Fittings from the Earliest Times to the End of the Eighteenth Century* (Cambridge: The University Press, 1901); George Haven Putnam, *Books and Their Makers in the Middle Ages* (New York: G. P. Putnam's Sons, 1896–1897; 2 volumes), I, 133–145; and, despite their specialized themes, Léopold Delisle, *Le cabinet des manuscrits de la Bibliothèque Impériale; étude sur la formation de ce dépôt, comprenant les éléments d'une histoire de la calligraphie, de la miniature, de la reliure, et du commerce des livres à Paris avant l'invention de l'imprimerie* (Paris: Imprimerie impériale,

1868–1881; 3 volumes), and Wilhelm Wattenbach, *Das Schrift-wesen im Mittelalter* (Leipzig: S. Hirzel, 1896; 3rd edition).

3. Even demanded of royalty, *e. g.*, by the Faculty of Medicine at Paris from Louis XI. See Frederick Sommer Merryweather, *Bibliomania in the Middle Ages* (London: The Woodstock Press, 1933), p. 34.

4. British Museum, Department of Egyptian and Assyrian Anti-quities, *A Guide to the Babylonian and Assyrian Antiquities* (Lon-don: Printed by Order of the Trustees, 1908; 2nd edition), p. 41, and C. Bezold, "Bibliotheks- und Schriftwesen im alten Ninive," *Zentralblatt für Bibliothekswesen*, XXI (1904), 2.

5. *Rufini Presbyteri prologus in libros* ΠΕΡΙ ΑΡΧΩΝ *Origenis Presbyteri*, p. 114, *in* J.-P. Migne, ed., *Patrologiae cursus completus* (Paris, 1844–1900; 221 volumes), series graeca, v. XI.

6. Heinrich Meisner, "Der Bücherfluch," *Zeitschrift für Bücher-freunde*, I, pt. 1 (1897), 101–102.

7. British Museum, Department of Oriental Printed Books and Manuscripts, *Catalogue of Syriac Manuscripts in the British Mu-seum Acquired since the Year 1838*, by William Wright (London, 1870–1872; 3 parts), III, 1100. In Part I, manuscripts XVII, LXXXVIII, and CX have similar anathemas. See also reviews by Th. Nöldeke and Geiger in *Zeitschrift der Deutschen Morgenländ-ischen Gesellschaft*, XXV (1871), 266–276, and Paul de Lagarde, "Die Handschriftensammlung des Grafen Ashburnham," *Nach-richten von der Königlichen Gesellschaft und der Georg-Augusts-Universität zu Göttingen*, 1884, p. 22.

8. XXIX.

9. Karl Emich Philipp Wilhelm Franz, Graf zu Leiningen-Westerburg (Neu-Leiningen), *German Book-Plates; an Illustrated Handbook of German and Austrian Exlibris*, translated by G. Ravenscroft Dennis (London: G. Bell and Sons, 1901), p. 49.

10. *Op. cit.*, p. 529; cited from Cod. gr. monac. 544.

11. Lagarde, *loc. cit.*, and G. A. Crüwell, "Die Verfluchung der Bücherdiebe," *Archiv für Kulturgeschichte*, IV (1906), 206.

12. Dom Michel Félibien, *Histoire de l'Abbaye Royale de Saint-Denys en France* (Paris: Leonard, 1706), "Pièces justificatives," no. 2.

13. Full text in August Reifferscheid, "Bibliotheca patrum latinorum, v.-IX., italica," *Sitzungsberichte der Akademie der Wis-senschaften* (*Vienna*), philologisch-historische Klasse, LXX (1872), 88; see also Wattenbach, *op. cit.*, p. 531. For the explanation of the curious word Maranatha see J. H. Thayer, "Maranatha," in James Hastings, ed., *A Dictionary of the Bible* (New York: Scrib-ner, 1902; 4 volumes), III, 241–243.

14. Cited in Crüwell, *op. cit.*, p. 209, and E. G. Vogel, "Die

Bibliothek der Benedictiner Abtei Reichenau," *Serapeum*, III (1842), 6.

15. France, Bibliothèque Nationale, Département des Manuscrits, *Catalogue des manuscrits des fonds Libri et Barrois*, by Léopold Delisle (Paris, 1888), p. 30.

16. Clark, *op. cit.*, p. 74; Thompson, *op. cit.*, p. 627; and Léopold Delisle, "Documents sur les livres et les bibliothèques au moyen âge," *Bibliothèque de l'École des Chartes*, XI (1849; also numbered 3rd series, v. I), 216–231.

17. Clark, *op. cit.*, p. 56.

18. Léopold Delisle, *Le cabinet des manuscrits de la Bibliothèque Impériale*, I, 44–46.

19. Leiningen-Westerburg, *op. cit.*, p. 48–49. Urban VIII and Innocent XII were among the pontiffs who issued decrees against book thieves, according to evidence uncovered by Nisiar, "Ex-libris contre les voleurs de livres et les emprunteurs négligents." *Intermédaire des chercheurs et curieux*, LVII (20 January 1908), 80.

20. *Ibid.* The full title is quoted by Leiningen-Westerburg in his "Zum Kapitel vom 'Bücherfluch,'" *Zeitschrift für Bücherfreunde*, I, pt. 2 (1897), 431.

21. Reproduced in Heinrich Lempertz, *Bilderhefte zur Geschichte des Bücherbandes und der mit demselben verwandten Künste und Gewerbe* (Cologne: I. M. Heberle, H. Lempertz, 1853–1865; 13 annual parts), 1859, Tafel IV, plate 3.

22. Maurice Prou, *Manuel de paléographie latine et française* (Paris: A. Picard, 1910; 3rd edition), p. 112–113.

23. Bernard de Montfaucon, *Palaeographia Graeca* (Paris: L. Guérin, J. Boudot, and C. Robustet, 1708), p. 75. See also p. 58, 63, 69, 76, 89, 230, 292, and 385.

24. Edmond Locard, "La mort de Judas Iscariote; étude critique d'exégèse et de médecine légale, sur un cas de pendaison célèbre," *Archives d'anthropologie criminelle de médecine légale et de psychologie normale et pathologique*, XIX (1904), 421–454, and A. Wrede, "Judas Ischarioth," *in* Hanns Bächtold-Stäubli, ed., *Handwörterbuch des deutschen Aberglaubens* (Berlin, Walther de Gruyter, 1927–41; v. I-IX), IV, 800–808.

25. XLII (1921), 234–252.

26. K. Solovev, *K legendam ob Iudye predatelye* (Kharkov, 1908), p. 104, note 1 quoting from Otcêt Imper. Pub. Bibl. 1883, 1. 184.

27. *Sachsenspiegel: Land- und Lehnrecht*, edited by Karl August Eckhardt (Hannover: Hahnsche Buchhandlung, 1933; 2 volumes; *Monumenta Germaniae historica. Fontes iuris Germanici antiqui*, n. s., v. I), I, 11 (lines 221–248).

28. *Vorlesungen über die Kunde hebräischer Handschriften*,

deren Sammlungen und Verzeichnisse (Leipzig: Otto Harrassowitz, 1897; *Beiheft zum Centralblatt für Bibliothekswesen*, v. xix), p. 41.

29. *German Book-Plates*, p. 48.

30. *Op. cit.*, p. 213, note 7. Crüwell's reference to Goldzieher is incorrect, and it has not been possible to verify it.

31. *Op. cit.*, p. 102.

32. *Ibid.*, p. 220, note 1; cited from Schukowitz on "Der Bücherfluch" in the *Grazer Volksblatt*, 1900, no. 39.

33. Christian Friedrich Wilhelm Jacobs and Friedrich August Ukert, *Beiträge zur älteren Litteratur; oder, Merkwürdigkeiten der Herzogl. öffentlichen Bibliothek zu Gotha* (Leipzig: Dyk, 1835–1843; 6 parts in 3 volumes), ii, 12.

34. *Kloster Admont und seine Beziehungen zur Wissenschaft und zum Unterricht* (Brno: Im Selbstverlag des Verfassers, 1892), p. 213.

35. "Altschlesische Schreibverse," *Mitteilungen der Schlesischen Gesellschaft für Volkskunde*, xix (1917), 27–28.

36. Students at a well-known university in Cambridge, Mass., also make light of a book-plate inscription in many of their library's books. As a minatory device, the university has enumerated the number of years done by the thief who once stole these books and was subsequently apprehended and convicted.

37. Merryweather, *loc. cit.*

38. Cod. lat. mon. 14,258; cited by Wattenbach, *op. cit.*, p. 527, with references to other sources where it may be found.

39. Wattenbach, *op. cit.*, p. 533. For Dathan and Abiram see Numbers, xvi, 30–32.

40. Cod. Lyon. 463 (saec. ix), cited by Crüwell, *op. cit.*, p. 215, note 1.

41. Leiningen-Westerburg, *German Book-Plates*, p. 45.

42. Wattenbach, *op. cit.*, p. 534.

43. *Ibid.*, p. 533.

44. W. J. Hardy, *Book-Plates* (London: Kegan, Paul, Trench, Trübner, and Co., 1897), p. 163.

45. J. J. C., "Fly-leaf Scribblings." *Notes and Queries*, ser. 2, iv (10 October 1857), 284.

46. W. Jaggard "Book Borrowers," *Notes and Queries*, ser. 12, vii (30 April 1921), 351.

47. A. R. Waller, "Book Borrowers," *Notes and Queries*, ser. 12, viii (26 March 1921), 2.

48. Mary Bateson, Review of "*Bibliothèque de la Faculté des Lettres. III. Mélanges d'Histoire du Moyen Âge.* Publiée sous la direction de M. le Professeur Luchaire. (Paris: Alcan. 1897.)," *English Historical Review*, xiii (1898), 138.

49. "Book Inscription," *Notes and Queries*, ser. 9, I (29 January 1898), 86.

50. Philip Norman. "Lines to Book Borrowers," *Notes and Queries*. ser. 9, XII (29 August 1903), 167.

51. John Byrne Leicester Warren (Lord de Tabley), *A Guide to the Study of Book-Plates (Ex-Libris)* (Manchester: Sherratt and Hughes, 1900) p. 97.

52. *Ibid*.

53. G. O., "Un curieux ex-libris," *Revue des bibliothèques et archives de Belgique*, II (1904), 403.

54. Meisner, *op. cit.*, p. 103.

55. *Ibid*.

56. Leiningen-Westerburg, *German Book-Plates*, p. 45.

57. Hardy, *op. cit.*, p. 168.

58. Franciscus Sweertius, *Selectae christiani orbis deliciae* (Cologne, 1608), p. 571. See also Robert Pierpont, "Book-stealing: Degrees of Blackness," *Notes and Queries*, ser. 10, VIII (14 December 1907), 475–476, and O. Walde, "Henrik Rantzaus bibliotek och dess öden," *Nordisk tidskrift för bok- och biblioteksväsen*, I (1914), 181–192.

59. Leiningen-Westerburg, "Zum Kapitel vom Bücherfluch," *loc. cit.*, p. 432.

60. Leiningen-Westerburg, *German Book-Plates*, p. 47, and Arthur Mayall, "A Rhyming Warning to Book Borrowers," *Notes and Queries*, ser. 9, II (5 November 1898), 376.

61. Tenebrae, "A Rhyming Warning to Book Borrowers," *Notes and Queries*, ser. 9, II (5 November 1898), 376.

62. F. Wilson Dobbs, "A Riming Warning for Book Borrowers," *Notes and Queries*, ser. 9, IV (19 August 1899) 154.

63. Walter Hamilton, *French Book-Plates* (London, G. Bell and Sons, 1896), p. 9.

64. F. W. R., "Inscriptions in Books," *Notes and Queries*, ser. 1, X (14 October 1854) 309.

65. "Ex-libris contre les voleurs de livres et les emprunteurs négligents," *Intermédiaire des chercheurs et curieux*, LVI (20 October 1907) col. 579–580.

66. Quoted by Patrick Maxwell, "A Rhyming Warning to Book-Borrowers," *Notes and Queries*, ser. 9, II (6 August 1898), 115.

67. A tremendous anathema uncovered in a Harleian manuscript to the great glee of nineteenth-century book folk. See W. Sparrow Simpson, "Inscriptions in Books," *Notes and Queries*, ser. 1, X (10 October 1854), 309.

68. *loc. cit.*

69. J. P. B., "Book Inscription," *Notes and Queries*, ser. 4, VI (9 July 1860), 26.

70. Dobbs, *loc. cit.*

71. R. Denny Urlin, "A Rhyming Warning to Book Borrowers," *Notes and Queries,* ser. 9, I (25 June 1898), 513.

72. Henry Attwell, "A Rhyming Warning to Book Borrowers," *Notes and Queries,* ser. 9, I (7 May 1898), 366.

73. *Ibid.,* p. 512.

74. *Ibid.* (note by John T. Page).

75. W. R. H., "Book-Stealing; Degrees of Blackness," *Notes and Queries,* ser. 10, VII (16 March 1909), 212.

76. Richard H. Thornton, "A Rhyming Warning to Book Borrowers," *Notes and Queries,* ser. 9, II (5 November 1898), 376.

77. Thomas Olive Mabbott, "Book Borrowers," *Notes and Queries,* CXLIX (11 July 1925), 33.

78. Leiningen-Westerburg, *German Book-Plates,* p. 48.

79. G. J. Boekenoogen, "Aanteekeningen van Boekeneigenaars," *Tijdschrift voor Boek- en Bibliotheekwezen,* II (1904), 215–216.

80. E. g., see R. W. G. Vail, "Seventeenth Century American Book Labels," *The American Book Collector,* IV (1933), 164–171.

81. Lord de Tabley, *op. cit.,* p. 100.

82. William Cushing Bamburg, "A Rhyming Warning to Book-Borrowers," *Notes and Queries,* ser. 9, II (5 November 1898), 376.

83. *Loc. cit.*

84. Leiningen-Westerburg, *German Book-Plates,* p. 47.

85. Crüwell, *op. cit.,* p. 222.

86. *Supra,* note 16.

Religatum de Pelle Humana

No, YOUR LOCAL PUBLIC LIBRARY doesn't have one. Nevertheless, if American librarianship is to be all things to all men,
some one of its practitioners should make some effort at least
to satisfy the intellectual curiosity of readers who would get
to the bottom of the matter once and for all. I refer to the
problem of anthropodermic bibliopegy, a subject which haunts
the world of bookmen and not infrequently finds its way into
the columns of their journals as a sly rumor. But he who is
determined to get at the real story will discover that the
macabre art of leatherwork in the tanned human integument
has a long history as folklore and propaganda in addition to
the more "refined" traditions created by the bibliopegistic
dandies of the nineteenth century.

The custom of flaying the sacrilegious and tanning their
impious hides has roots in Greek antiquity. According to
Phrygian legend, the Silenus Marsyas, god of the river of the
same name, made so bold as to challenge Apollo to a contest
with the lyre and, upon losing, suffered the indignity of being
flayed.[1] Apollo hung the skin in the market place at Celaenae,
and it was still being shown there in Xenophon's day. Ctesip-
pus did not approve of the disposition of Marsyas' mortal
remains; for Plato makes him say in *Euthydemus*[2]: "They may
skin me alive, if only my skin is made at last, not like that of
Marsyas, into a leathern bottle, but into a piece of virtue."

Herodotus[3] advised that the Scythians made covers for their
quivers, cloaks, and "napkins" (χειρόμακτρον) of human skin;
and he goes on to say that they went to the extreme of flaying
the entire body, even to the finger nails, and stretching the
tanned skin upon a wooden frame (διατείναντε ἐπί ξύλωυ) for

119

exhibition as a trophy. Cambyses ordered the flaying of Sisamnes, father of Otanes, and his skin stretched across the seat of the throne on which he sat in judgment. The son, who succeeded his father by special dispensation, was enjoined to remember what he was sitting on when making his decisions. (Herodotus, v, 25).

Our Anglo-Saxon forebears were no less savage in their treatment of marauding Danes who violated their places of worship. The early volumes of *Notes and Queries* are full of references to human skin nailed to church doors in Hadstock, Copford, Worcester, Southwark, Rochester, and elsewhere.[4] Samuel Pepys was not merely propagating idle rumor when he wrote on April 10, 1661: "To Rochester, and there saw the Cathedral; then away thence observing the great doors of the church, as they say, covered with the skins of the Danes." The human skin nailed to the doors of St. Saviour's Church in Southwark was in the Guildhall Museum before the Blitz[5]; but it is altogether possible that the unknown Teutonic marauder to whom it once belonged has met with final destruction at the hands of one of his own descendants. Gilbert Scott found the skins of robbers which Edward i had nailed on the door of the Chapel of the Pyx in Westminster Abbey as posthumous punishment for abstracting the royal treasure.[6] Frank Buckland, the nineteenth-century naturalist whose father was dean of Westminster, has told the story that in his own day a piece of hard dry skin was found underneath the bossed head of a huge iron nail that was fixed upon the door of the Abbey's Chapter House. John Quekett, then assistant conservator of the museum of the Royal College of Surgeons, recognized it as the skin of a blond person, probably by discovery of vestigal remnants of hair by means of microscopic examination.[7]

Folk beliefs which may have their roots in times which we do not care to recall in all their details are full of human skin legends. German Swiss peasants relate that a wicked shepherd was once skinned by spirits and his skin spread out on the roof of an Alpine hut.[8] Gypsy legend tells of a fair princess who was turned into an old woman and placed in solitary confinement with her skin hung in a secret room; but she was finally released from her curse when a generous youth paid court to her.[9]

A widespread medieval belief that girdles of human skin aided in childbirth was gleefully repeated by those pornographers *par excellence*, Herman Ploss and Max and Paul Bartels.[10]

The ancient Nordic peoples were fascinated by the notion of slipping out of one's skin.[11] One Icelandic yarn tells of a girl who stepped out of the soles of her feet and made seven-league boots of them with which she could travel over land and sea. Another Scandinavian saga tells of a thrall who was bound to serve his master until his shoes wore out, but the latter, being made of human skin, were indestructible. It was held to be fatal ever to step on hallowed ground (premises of churches and cemeteries) with such foot-wear. A lucky six-pence was readily available to the Norseman who had breeches made out of human skin, and not infrequently two friends entered into a bargain agreeing that the first who died would surrender his skin to the other for appropriate use. Unfortunately, once the pants are donned, they grow to the body. The lucky sixpence itself had to be stolen from a poverty-stricken widow during the reading of the Gospels in a church. The only way to get rid of these devil's breeches was to persuade some other witless materialist to take them over; and once the latter had his right leg in the left side of the enchanted pants, he would never be free of his malefactor until he got the other leg in the right side. Another widespread superstition in the ancient North held that a magic carpet could be made from the dorsal skin of a dead man. Reminiscent of the sacrilegious aspects of these heathen Scandinavian beliefs is the passage in *Là-bas* where J. K. Huysmans gloats on a book binding in the skin of an unbaptized infant with a panel stamp representing a Host blessed in the Black Mass.[12]

By way of warning to British and American law enforcement officers in Germany, it is suggested that the manufacture of anthropodermic girdles be made a penal offense inasmuch as medieval Germans argued that such a garment was the password to lykanthropy.[13]

But even Jerry believes in punishment of the wicked, for a legend from the Upper Palatinate holds that the Devil took the skin of a wicked landlord who had "skinned" his own tenants without mercy (if we may be permitted to translate in this manner the German pun on *schinden*, which has the double meaning of "flay" and "oppress.") A Count von Erbach of Odenwald in Hessia ordered sportsman's breeches to be made out of his skin after his death; and another charming Hessian custom was the manufacture of belts, suspenders, and knife sheaths from the booty of blood feuds.[14]

The medieval man also liked to toy with the idea of human parchment as a medium for writing. It has been alleged that one Mexican calendar on human parchment is in the Saxon State Library in Dresden and that another is in Vienna, but there is no evidence that the Aztecs were familiar with this aspect of the art.[15] The Japanische Palais, quondam home of the Sächsiche Landesbibliothek, is now a pile of rubble, and surviving staff members have indicated that they have more important tasks than to answer queries of curious Americans. I am personally inclined to believe that the beautiful thirteenth century Bible in the Bibliothèque Nationale (fonds Sorbonne no. 1297) is on parchment from a still-born Irish lamb, as Gayet de Sansale maintained, rather than on *peau de femme*, as the Abbé Rive would have us believe. Nevertheless, the sage Gayet advised that another thirteenth century Bible which was in his custody (fonds Sorbonne no. 1625) and a text of the Decretals (fonds Sorbonne no. 1625) were written on human skin.[16]

Alfred Franklin gossiped after Granier de Cassagnac's questionable pamphlet on the Directory that some copies of one edition of the French Constitution were written or printed on human skin.[17]

But one of the most astounding tales is that of the wandering Icelander Jón Olafsson ("Indiafári") who gravely tries to pawn off the story of three anthropodermic books owned by a Coromandel Coast sorcerer.[18] Allegedly they were written on a special kind of parchment three centuries old. This parchment was of human skin, and pull as one might, it would always spring back into its proper shape. The elasticity of human skin will be verified by any of us who may have been raised in a small town in the South and can remember the local Negro who could get four golf balls inside of his mouth at one time. A. M. Villon says that an eighteenth century glutton named Tarare could get twelve eggs and twelve apples into his mouth.[19]

Beginning in the Middle Ages and going on through the seventeenth century, the notion of completely tanned human skins has kept a firm hold on the medical as well as the lay mind. How many of us have not heard the tale of some "leather general" that a pilgrim to the centers of Kultur has found (probably the ones in the Zittauer Ratsbibliothek,[20] the University of Basel's Museum of Natural History, or the University of Göttingen)? M. Ulric-Richard Desaix, a direct descendant of the famous general of the First French Republic, informed the anonymous authority who wrote for the *Chronique Médicale*[21] that in 1874 he saw a whole human hide of a thirty-year-old man at a country fair in Châteauroux and that subsequently that same hide was exhibited in Le Havre in an "Anthropological, Anatomical, and Ethnological Museum."

The vault of the church of Poppelsdorf (near Bonn) is said to contain the dried (not mummified) bodies of some twenty monks in full cowl and cassock[22]; and the Capuchin Convent in Valetta preserved a number of desiccated former inmates.[23] Another yarn picked up by an Englishman on his *grand tour* tells of "the cave" adjoining a church in Bordeaux containing about seventy "perfectly tanned" human bodies.[24] In 1684 Sir Robert Viner, that loyal alderman of London, gave Bodley's Library a tanned human skin as well as a human skeleton and the dried body of a Negro boy.[25] His generosity was matched by William Harvey who gave the College of Physicians a tanned human skin. Another fully tanned skin is in the Physiological Museum of the Lyceum of Versailles. A Dr. Downing of Stourbridge preserved in a sumac solution the entire skin of William Waite, executed in Worcester about 1826 for murder.[26] Edouard Harlé reported that he had seen in the Museo Zootécnico of Barcelona the tanned skins of a Negro man and a white woman.[27]

One of the most fanciful tales that the Middle Ages can offer on the tanning of human skin is that of the Hussite General John Ziska. Robert Burton put the incident to good rhetorical use: "As the great Captain Zisca would have a drum made of his skin when he was dead, because he thought the very noise of it would put his enemies to flight, I doubt not but these following lines, when they shall be recited, or hereafter read, will drive away melancholy (though I be gone) as much as Zisca's drum could terrify his foes."[28]

Johann Staricius' *Neuvermehrter Heldenschatz*[29] is one of the earliest complete accounts of this somewhat doubtful but nonetheless colorful story, and Staricius probably found the tale in some more extensive Czech account. Carlyle condemned the story as "fabulous, though in character with Ziska" in his biography of Frederick the Great.[30] The grossly vulgar *Tetoniana* of G. J. Witkowski has a fanciful illustration of Ziska's drum indicating that it was made of the skin of his chest.[31] Walter Hart Blumenthal and Paul Kersten try to convince their readers that the "Janizary drum" made of Ziska's skin in presently in the Bavarian Armee-Museum, although it has been almost three-quarters of a century now since Gustave Pawlowski informed the gullible that the Bohemian historian Palacky had disproved the legend.[32] Ziska was emulated in the rather mock heroic gesture of a French Republican (a royalist according to Essad Bey) who fell at Nantes in 1793. He ordered a drum to be made of his tanned skin. His skin was indeed tanned, even to his nails, and preserved in the Nantes Museum of Natural History, but no drum was ever made of it.[33]

Apropos of Witkowski's version of Ziska's drum, it is worth

only a passing note to call attention to the erotomaniacs who have played with the human hide in their own peculiar way. Isidore Liseux, the nineteenth-century Parisian publisher of erotic books, and the Goncourt brothers[34] started enough rumors about this sort of thing to keep the devotees of the *Intermédiaire* busy for two generations. Lest anyone doubt the wildest tales of erotic bibliopegy, he need only consult Ernest de Crauzat's investigation of modern French binding.

Many physicians have wallets and cigarette cases which are remininscent of unsuccessful professional activity (and/or unpaid bills?). The nineteenth-century doorkeeper of the anatomical classroom in the College of Edinburgh used to carry a pocket-book made of the skin of the murderer of William Burke[35] who was executed in that city in 1829 (for "Burkeing") and, in wax effigy, used to terrify visitors to pre-Hitler London at Mme. Tussaud's. In 1937 Mr. W. F. Kaynor, president of the Waterbury Button Company, presented the U.S. National Museum with a piece of leather from human skin and a billfold made from the grain surface of such leather. A billfold known far and wide in upper New York State may be found in the bar of Rattlesnake Pete in Rochester, where it rests in archival repose on the basis of a rumor that it is made of a Negro's skin. A cuirass with straps and other accessories was made from the beautifully tatooed skin of a convict who died at the penitentiary at St. Mary á la Comte in the middle of the last century.[36] The Centennial Exposition in Philadelphia in 1876 was a happy hunting ground for the devotees of articles from anthropodermic leather. Besides a pack of forty playing cards allegedly made of human leather and taken by the U.S. Army as loot from an Indian tribe, there was also a small pair of boots whose tops were made of human skin. The latter were exhibited by the manufacturers. M. and A. Mahrenholz of New York, and were subsequently presented to the U.S. National Museum.

Footwear has played an important role in the history of the industrial use of human leather in America. The most famous incident involving anthropodermic footwear was the notorious

Tewksbury affair which caused a great rumpus in Massachusetts after the supervisory board of the Tewksbury Almshouse had been suspended by Governor Benjamin F. Butler on April 23, 1883. It was charged that practical use had been made of the tanned hides of deceased inmates, part of whose mortal remains had allegedly been sold to local tanners serving the shoe industry. According to a galley sheet entitled "Human Hide Industry," a copy of which is in the Surgeon-General's Library in Washington, General Butler charged that the human hide industry had attained national proportions and that it had even reached the point where the peculiar styles of tanning the human integument had caused as much jealousy between Vermont, New Hampshire, and Massachusetts as the formula for the mint julep has caused between Georgia and Kentucky.

The galley in question is a statement by William Muller, tanner of North Cambridge, who effectively denies the charges of General Butler as a political farce. Nevertheless, the matter was taken so seriously that, according to the Massachusetts *House Journal* of July 23, 1883, a Mr. Mellen of Worcester asked leave to introduce a bill to make the tanning of human hide illegal, but on July 27, 1883, permission to introduce it was refused.

A pair of high-heeled lady's shoes made from an executed criminal (inspected by Henry Stephens)[37], three complete human skins (one dressed like parchment)[38], and a shirt made of a man's entrails (according to R. W. Hackwood) once graced Hermann Boerhaave's surgical collection in his museum in Leyden. A pair of gloves immortalized part of a soldier named Steptoe who was executed early in the last century at the same gaol where Oscar Wilde later paid his debt to society.[39] In 1887, after the criminal Pranzini had been executed for his notorious murders of *femmes galantes*, two card cases were made of his skin and presented by Inspector Rossignol to Messrs. Taylor and Goron, chief and number one man respectively of the Sûreté. The original piece of skin removed from Pranzini's body was about forty centimeters square and was tanned by Destresse of Paris. However, the Parisian constabulary never had the opportunity to gape at these police trophies, for the solicitor who handled the case denounced Rossignol and ordered the card cases burned.[40]

But the French had been using human skin for wearing apparel even during the *ancien régime*. According to J. C. Valmont de Bomare, the royal surgeon Pierre Sue, father of Eugène, contributed to the Cabinet du Roi a pair of slippers made of human skin; and in the same museum, says Valmont, was a belt on which the vestige of a human nipple was plainly evident.[41] James Lane Allen's often reprinted essay on "The Blue-Grass Region of Kentucky" reports that Hawthorne conversed with an old man in England who advised him that the Kentuckians flayed Tecumseh where he fell and converted his skin into razor-straps.

Isolated bits of human skin serving no useful purpose are found in many collections. In 1884 G. S. Knapp of Chicago presented the U.S. National Museum with a small piece of leather which he said was taken from the back of the neck of the Indian Chief, "Cut Nose," who participated in the "New Uhlm Massacre" (New Ulm, Minnesota) of 1862 and was reported to have slaughtered thirty-two women and children with his own hands. In the museum of the Philosophical Institution at Reading (England) there was once a small portion of the skin of Jeremy Bentham, which allegedly "bore a close resemblance to a yellow and shrivelled piece of parchment."[42] This relic recalls the joint of Galileo's backbone in the museum of Padua which was surreptitiously abstracted by the ghoulish physician entrusted with the transfer of the scientist's remains to Santa Cruce in Florence in 1737. According to Mr. Cecil B. Hurry, sub-librarian of Trinity College, Cambridge, there are two small pieces of human skin in the Newton Cabinet of the Trinity College Library, *viz.*, (1) a piece in color said to be from the murderer William Corder (executed in 1828), known to all lovers of high melodrama as the slayer of Marie Marten in the Red Barn, and (2) a cream-colored bit from the murderer Thomas Weems who expired at Cambridge in 1819. It is notorious that the Public Library of that shrine of bibliophiles, Bury St. Edmunds, contains the complete trial proceedings against Corder bound in the rest of his skin, which was tanned by the same surgeon who also prepared his skeleton for the West Suffolk Hospital.[43] I myself once owned a dried Indian head won from a Pan-American pilot in a poker game in Oaxaca a few years back, but the head showed no evidence of any of the recognized processes of tanning and tawing.

A widely gossiped incident about a piece of human skin that was never tanned has been properly told by Mr. H. W. Tribolet of the Extra Binding Department of R. R. Donnelley and Sons in Chicago. Some time ago, probably about 1932, Alfred DeSauty, who was instructing the bookbinders of the Lakeside Press in Chicago, gave a talk on bookbinding before a mixed group of interested people. When he came to anthropodermic bindings, he stated in jest that he would be quite happy to be able to bind a copy of *Uncle Tom's Cabin* in a Negro's skin. His statement was hardly serious, and he soon forgot it. But shortly thereafter a clumsy looking package came to his office with his name on the address label. Inside was a portion of a Negro skin that had been taken from the body of a person who must had died only a few hours previously, for the skin was quite moist and flexible. The unwelcome gift was promptly dispatched to the boiler room. Many months afterwards it was revealed that a mortician's apprentice was in the audience at the time the original statement was made by DeSauty and, appreciating a good opportunity for his crude joke, sent the portion of the skin in question.

By this time it is not difficult to understand how the fact and fiction of the lore of human leather have become almost hopelessly entangled. As if to add to the confusion, political propagandists have captalized on the natural human abhorrence for the science to the extent of creating a whole system of folklore. But the use of human skin tales did not attain its full growth as a propagandistic weapon until the French Revolution.[44]

Believe, if you care to, the rumors of Philippe-Egalité's anthropodermic breeches made of one piece (probably of whole cloth).[45] Believe, if you will, the yarn about another lovable character from the same period who is said to have engineered the execution of his thieving maid, secured her body for flaying and tanning and had breeches made from the same. Upon subsequently being reminded of her delinquencies, so goes the tale, this ingenious moralist would slap his thigh and shout, "But here she is, the rogue. Here she is!"[46] The story probably may be traced to some contemporary Scandinavian adventurer in Paris who was dreaming of a lucky sixpence. Believe, if you will, the yarns spun about the famous tannery at Meudon by the Marquise de Créquy (Maurice Cousin), Georges Duval, F. S. Feuillet de Conches, Bibliophile Jacob (Paul Lacroix),[47] and countless others. Or believe the rhetoric of Carlyle in *Dr. Claudius* that the French nobles laughed at Rousseau's theories, but that their skins went to bind the second edition of his Social Contract.[48]

The French Revolution did produce books bound in human skin, but one must discount such impossible fictions as that of Feuillet de Conches to the effect that sample copies of *The Rights of Man* bound in leather from Meudon (which also provisioned the revolutionary armies, he alleged) were distributed to guests at a "Bal du Zéphir" held in a graveyard. M. Villenave did possess a copy of *The Rights of Man* bound in this material, and few of us who have made the *grand tour* have failed to visit the Musée Carnavalet and inspect the copy of the French Constitution of 1793. As I remember the latter it was light green in color (no doubt stained), and it looked like the skin of a suckling pig. It belonged successively to Villenave, Granier de Cassagnac (who, as we have seen, made a better thing out of an already good story), the Marquis de Turget, and finally the Carnavalet, which brought in 1889.

The yet unwritten unprejudiced history of the French Revolution will devote several chapters to this propaganda about the Meudon tannery. But far more vicious than the gaily macabre French Revolution and its rumor mongers was the abolitionist scuttlebutt that Southern slaveowners, as a token of "special affection" to favorite human chattel, would tan the skin of slaves after death and use it to bind the family Bible. In point of fact, the only recorded use of human skin during the War Between the States was by a yankee. Joseph Leidy's own copy of his *Elementary Treatise on Human Anatomy* is preserved in the Library of the College of Physicians in Philadelphia with the following inscription: "The leather with which this book is bound, is human skin, from a soldier who died during the great southern rebellion (*sic!*)." Southern historians about to write an impartial history of the War from the Southern point of view will take appropriate note of this damming bit of evidence.

During the first war between Germany and the rest of the civilized world both sides were guilty of fantastic propaganda about the use of skins of both their own dead and the enemy dead. In World War II we were still loath to believe the most commonplace Nazi atrocities because we simply could not swallow the impossible tale about the source of German fats and oils during the first war. Even neutrals made good use of public guillibility during World War I. According to those Arabs who had less respect for truth than the Prophet had, any "person of color" who fell on a European battlefield was flayed, and from his hide were prepared handsome brief cases destined for the use of diplomats who would draw up the peace treaties and bookbindings for learned tomes on the history of that war, the madness of the Occident.[49] Paul Kersten, famous German binder, who was the most adept of all his colleagues in human leather-work, actually made a brief case of part of a fellow mortal.[50]

Apropos of Paul Kersten, it is interesting to note that this impeccable artist who should have been above the pettiness of political rumors was involved in just such a scandal.[51] In 1913 Kersten placed on exhibition with the well known firm of Reuss and Pollack[52] in Berlin some twelve books[53] which he had bound in human skin. None were priced, but the dealers took it upon themselves to sell one of the volumes, *Die knöcherne Hand,* for RM 75.—without Kersten's permission. Kersten was quite indignant that his art should yield such miserly returns and immediately instituted a suit against Reuss and Pollack. The case dragged through the courts of Berlin, and numerous experts were called upon to testify concerning the value of such a volume. Prussian jurists carefully explained (and this is the true masterpiece of Imperial German propaganda) that Germany was a difficult place to decide such a suit inasmuch as all the experts were in France, citing in particular the Parisian dealer Dorbon, who had asked 600 francs for an anthropodermic binding. Ultimately the case was settled out of court with Reuss and Pollack indemnifying Kersten to the extent of RM 175.—as the difference between the price of the book and the value Kersten imputed to it. But the most fantastic aspect of this incident is the allegation of Kersten that the purchaser was the wife of the American ambassador. The Hon. James W. Gerard advises that Mrs. Gerard never purchased such a book, and he classes the story with the rumor that when Mrs. Gerard was given a Red Cross decoration by the German government, she pinned it to her dog's collar and paraded him on what used to be Unter den Linden. It has not been possible to ascertain whether Mrs. John G. A. Leishman, wife of Mr. Gerard's predecessor, was the purchaser of *Die knöcherne Hand.*

During the last war there were innumerable rumors about the practical uses to which the Nazis put the skins of their victims. The wretches who died at Buchenwald are said to have reappeared frequently on a table in a "gute Stube" adorning a volume of *Mein Kampf*[54]; and such credence did the United Nations justices at Nuremberg place in these reports that pieces of leather alleged to be tanned human skin were admitted as evidence in the processes. It has further been alleged that the skin of tattooed inmates of the concentration camps appealed to Wehrmacht officers' wives as much as it did to the unnamed warden of St. Mary à la Comte. Kenneth L. Dixon, an AP staff writer, reported in a dispatch of May 22, 1945, that Karl Voelkner, SS Obersturmführer at Buchenwald, gave CIC agents a signed statement confessing that lamp-shades were made of the skins of his slaves. Somewhat more practical minded SS officers at Dachau are supposed to have skinned Russian prisoners and made gloves, saddles, and house slippers of their hides.[55]

One fears, however, that we are going a bit out of bounds after reflecting upon the innuendo of a statement by William J. Humphreys in the *Herald-Tribune* for Feb. 2, 1945, on Nazi medical experiments with their prisoners: "What happened to the boiled human flesh the witness did not know, but he suspected that some use was made of it. It was collected in tins and carried away."

Getting back to the facts, it is of considerable interest to find out just what human leather looks like. Unfortunately (for those who would like to believe the mythology of Meudon) the formula allegedly used by French tanners of the Revolution has not been preserved. But Valmont de Bomaro has provided us with one formula, according to which the skin is saturated in a strong solution of alum, roman vitriol, and table salt for several days. Subsequently it is dried in the shade and dressed in the usual manner. Paul Kersten, like Dr. Downing, recommends sumac specifically as a medium for tanning human skin.

There is some disagreement as to the actual appearance of human leather. Paul Kersten says that the grain is quite remarkable, being a combination of coarse grained goat and pig skin. The back has the coarser grain whereas the chest and belly have a finer grain. The thickness of Kersten's skins was 2 mm (dorsal) and 1 mm (lateral). He stated that the consistency was considerably greater than in other leathers and that it is difficult to work because of the depth of the grain as in pigskin. Otherwise, Kersten argues, it is like fine morocco, and the amateur would mistake it for such. Americans who would verify Kersten's statements may inspect his handicraft in the binding of a set of papers of L'Admiral, formerly in the collection of Hans Friedenthal and presently in the Lane Medical Library of Stanford University. Dr.

Nathan van Patten, professor of bibliography at Stanford University, has confirmed the rumor that the doublures of this volume are of "graveyard" mole.

A. M. Villon authoritatively states that human skin can be tanned to both harsh-dry and soft-glossy states. He says that its color varies from the palest pink to the deepest brown, and that its thickness varies from a seventieth to a sixth of an inch, the greatest thickness being found over the belly. When tanned, Villon says, it increases in thickness and yields a very tough leather, fine-grained and quite soft. Holbrook Jackson agrees with Villon that human skin increases in thickness and yields a fine-grained, soft leather; and he goes on to quote Cyril Davenport to the effect that it resembles thick calf, although it is difficult to rid it completely of hair. The canard about the resemblance of human leather to calf may probably be traced to the English bibilophile Herbert Slater, and it has been effectively denied in the *Berliner Tageblatt*.[56] Jackson cites another unnamed authority who contends that it is more like sheep with a firm and close texture, soft to the touch, and susceptible of a fine polish. The anatomist of bibliomania examined a specimen tanned by Edwin Zaehnsdorf and concluded that it resembled morocco rather than pigskin. A notable piece in the Boston Athenaeum (*infra*) is said to resemble gray deerskin. Percy Fitzgerald said that the human skin of his acquaintance was "darker and more mottled than vellum."

The effect of tanning on the thickness of human skin is described by a Dr. Legrain of Villejuif, who confessed a quarter of a century ago to the editer of the *Mercure de France* that he had removed a piece of skin from a corpse while a student in medical school and had had it tanned. When it was returned to him six months after he had delivered it to the tanner, it had a "fearful solidity, completely shrivelled up." It was less than half the size of the original skin, but its thickness had increased to a full centimeter. The rigidity was greater than that of any skin he had ever seen before; and in order to put it in suitable condition for binding a book (Théophile Gautier's *Comédie de la mort*), he had to have it split to more pliable thickness.[57]

Of course, Gustav Bogeng (who owned a duodecimo in human skin by Kersten) could not refrain from adding his categorical finalities to the issue. He advised that the natural grain of human skin could readily be distinguished, even in the absence of vestigial hairs, from pig and goat skin and that it could be tanned so as to produce whatever grain might be desired. Bogeng solemnly warned his loyal disciples in the *Zeitschrift der Bücherfreunde* that any enthusiast who felt compelled to own an anthropodermic binding should protect himself by having a microscopic examination made of the merchandise.

Some of the wilder speculations on human skin have described it as soft and white (*peau de femme* according to the *American Weekly*); and a few authorities have speculated on the relative softness of human leather from various parts of the body, alleging that the softest comes from the thighs. On the other hand, the catalogue of the Le Havre fair's "Anthropological, Anatomical, and Ethnological Museum"[58] says that leather from the thighs is the thickest. Maurice Cousin's Marquise de Créquy alleged that human skin had a greater consistency than chamois but that the softness of the tissue deprived it of solidity. One of the few experts who has observed any resemblance of human skin to that of the higher anthropoids is Dard Hunter, who found that the human skin with which he operated resembled "in texture the skin of a monkey, and to some extent, pig skin." Hunter's story is too good to put on ice for a later paragraph.[59]

Some forty years ago, as a young man, the noted founder of the M.I.T. Paper Museum was learning the graphic arts in Elbert Hubbard's Roycroft Shop in East Aurora, N.Y. One day a widow of tender years presented him with a testimonial volume of letters addressed to her late husband and requested specifically that Hunter bind it in a leather which she herself would provide.

Hunter had been prepared to clothe the letters in his

choicest leather, but the customer supplied him with a piece that resembled neither the crushed levant nor the oasis niger which he reserved for his finer work. The lady did not hesitate to admit that the leather came from the back of the honoree of the letters. When Hunter learned that the lady remarried shortly thereafter, he speculated as to whether the lady's second husband would gaze at the memorial volume on the drawing room table and think of himself as a possible volume two; and, as the binder, Hunter annotated the incident with a heartfelt epilogue, "Let us hope that this was strictly a limited edition." Hunter writes that a half a century has erased from his memory the name of the lady for whom this extraordinary job was performed.

Extensive research fails to reveal that human skin was used for bookish purposes prior to the eighteenth century despite arguments of Gayet de Sansale and Villon. One is constrained to question the latter's undocumented statement that alchemists were "very fond of tanning small pieces of human skin, wherewith to bind their books of secrets, or prayer books." Perhaps the earliest plausible report of an anthropodermic binding comes from the indefatigable traveller and bibliophile Zacharias Conrad von Uffenbach.[60] Besides sundry stuffed human skins which he discovered in the course of his travels, he was particularly delighted to find an anthropodermic binding in the library of the Syndic of Maastricht in Bremen: "We also saw a little duodecimo, Molleri manuale praeparationis ad mortem. There seemed to be nothing remarkable about it, and you couldn't understand why it was here until you read in the front that it was bound in human leather. This unusual binding, the like of which I had never before seen, seemed especially well adapted to this book, dedicated to more meditation about death. You would take it for pig skin."

The earliest authentic example of an anthropodermic binding which has been identified is located in the library of the University of California at Los Angeles. It is the *Relation des mouvemens de la ville de Messine despuis l'année M. DC.*

LXXI. jusques à présent with an inscription running "À la Bibliothèque de M. Bignon. Reliure en peau humaine." A recent hand noted that the Bignon in question was Armand Jerome Bignon, librarian of Louis XV. But here we are plunged into folklore again; for there have been consistent but unconfirmed reports of books which Louis XV had bound in the skin of ex-mistresses, evidently "the skin you love to touch." Pre-revolutionary anthropodermic bindings will be a likely thesis topic for some inspired candidate for an advanced degree in a graduate library school.

Whether the practice of binding books in human skin was given its main impetus by the French Revolution is difficult to ascertain. There are other indications, and possibly more reliable ones than the tales propagated by Royalist historians, which point to the invention and cultivation of anthropodermic binding by the medical profession with the able seconding of their professional brethren practicing before the bar. We can be reasonably sure of the story told by Frognall Dibdin (for all his other weaknesses for the bibliographically sensational) to the effect that the classicist, bibliophile, and scientist Dr. Anthony Askew had a *Treatise of Anatomy* bound in human skin even though the volume itself has disappeared from sight. Bogeng confused the tale of Askew's *Treatise* (incidentally, calling Askew a Russian)[61] with that of a Yorkshire witch variously called Mary Bateman, Patman, Bates, Ratman, Putnam, Batman, and Raiman by the inexact.

Her real name was Mrs. Mary Harker Bateman, and after her execution at York Castle in 1809 she was dissected at the General Infirmary at Leeds, her skin tanned and distributed in small pieces to various applicants. A book bound in this woman's skin was allegedly in the library of the Prince of Wales at the Marlborough House at one time.[62] Another English physician, John Hunter (1728–1794) was supposed to have had a treatise on pathological dermatology bound up in a healthy cured human skin.[63]

The earliest anthropodermic binding prepared by a member of the medical profession and definitely known to exist at present is counted among the treasured relics of the Royal Infirmary at Bristol. In a cabinet near the skeleton of John Horwood, eighteen-year-old murderer hanged at Bristol New Drop in 1821, is a volume containing all the details of Horwood's crime, trial, execution and dissection. The book is bound in what would appear to be a light Russia, with tooled border lines in gold, a skull and crossbones in each corner, and the following gilt inscription in blackletter: "Cutis Vera Johannis Horwood."

Both the skeleton and the binding were prepared by Dr. Richard Smith, chief surgeon of the Infirmary for nearly half a century.[64] But the medicos of Bristol have no monopoly on the skins of executed criminals. Percy Fitzgerald stated that the Bristol Law Library also owned several volumes in the skins of local culprits which he saw in the shop of a dealer on St. Michael's Hill, Bristol, whence they had been sent for repair.[65]

It is difficult to fix the origins of the custom of flaying criminals and tanning their hides in England in modern times. Soldier Steptoe of Reading may enjoy the distinction of having been the first victim of this practice. A bit of the skin of one Cadwallader, executed at Hereford in 1816 for the murder of his wife in Leominster, was owned by a reader of *Notes and Queries* as late as 1873.[66] Charles Smith, the murderer, hanged at Newcastle-on-Tyne in 1817, underwent the process of posthumous flaying and tanning, and a part of his skin was placed *in* a book containing the particulars of his trial and execution. But the first authenticated case of a binding in a criminal's skin was Samuel Johnson's dictionary bound in the integument of one James Johnson (degree of relationship to the great lexigrapher unknown), publicly hanged on Castle Hill, Norwich, in 1818, before 5,000 spectators. The volume was owned by a Norwich bookseller named Muskett and subsequently passed to the possession of one of his brothers.[67] Mr. George Hayward, city librarian of Norwich, has been unable to locate the present whereabouts of this volume or to identify the Muskett family.

The disposal of the skin of Thomas Weems (executed in 1819) has already been noted. In 1824 one Thurtell was executed for the murder of Weare, and it is believed that a large roll of his skin, or, if not his, that of Arthur Thistlewood, the Cato Street conspirator, was in the possession of a fellow of Jesus College, Oxford, at one time during the last century.[68] It was said to have been admirably tanned and to resemble a very superior buckskin. Cantabs as well as Oxonians have displayed a fondness for anthropodermic binding. Cim alleged that one Queensby, a Greek scholar of Cambridge, ordered that upon his death he be flayed to provide a home for the *Iliad,* but it is not known whether his wishes were fulfilled.[69]

At least a part of William Burke's skin found its way into a library, even though not on the back of a book. After his execution, the publisher of his trial secured a portion of his skin, tanned it, and distributed small pieces to his clients. A portion of it, dyed dark blue, was placed in the extraordinary collection of papers relating to Burke and Hare which was formed for Walter Scott and placed in the library at Abbotsford.[70] In 1830, one year after Burke's execution, rat-catcher George Cudmore atoned with his life in the Devon County Jail for the murder of his spouse.[71] W. Clifford, book-seller of Exeter, somehow got hold of his skin after it had been tanned at the Devon and Exeter Hospital and used it years later to bind Tegg's edition of Milton (1852). This volume passed into the hands of the Exeter collector Ralph Sanders, and today it is in the Albert Memorial Library of that city.

In May, 1871, Lord H. haunted the boulevards and alleys of Paris for three days with a sizeable amount of pounds sterling in his pocket looking for an informant who would secure for him the cadaver of a female agitator who was to be executed by a firing squad. His intention was to flay the carcass and deliver the hide to the binder Trautz-Bauzonnet with instructions to use it to cover the two volumes of the first edition of *Le portier des chartreux.* But the hapless peer failed in his mission and received instead a slug of lead in his lower extremity which confined him to his bed for three months.[72]

It is possible that this story is a slightly distorted version of William Salt Brassington's tale of the agent of the London dealer who had an order for an anthropodermic binding for Holbein's *Dance of Death*. The agent betook himself to Paris during the Commune as the most likely source for his raw material, but he not only failed but also escaped only by the skin of his teeth from sharing the fate of the object of his search.[73]

In point of fact, there is only one example in France since the Revolution of a criminal whose hide was supposed to be tanned for the purpose of binding a book. The famed second story operator Campi, whose true name was never revealed to the public, was dissected after his execution, and his right side and arm were supposed to have been flayed to provide the leather for binding the account of his trial and dissection.

According to the *Chronique médicale*'s informants, M. Flandinette of the École d'anthropologie was to do the tanning. It has never been positively ascertained whether Campi's hide was actually used to bind his dossier, especially in view of the fact that its present whereabouts is unknown; but at all events it has come to light that a number of card cases were made of his skin and presented to various functionnaries of the Parisian constabulary. After the Campi incident, the criminal Pranzini was flayed and his hide tanned to amuse the Sûreté (supra). For the benefit of all concerned with American justice, let it be stated here and now that one of the few inside facts I can reveal about the F.B.I. is that the files of all our villains from Machine Gun Kelly to Herbert Hans Haupt are bound in plain flexible cardboard covers duly purchased on official vouchers. But our hands are by no means altogether clean.

This brings us to the most famous of all anthropodermic bindings, a strictly American product resting on the shelves of 10½ Beacon Street, the Boston Athenaeum. In February, 1944, the library letter of this venerable collection flung out a challenge captioned, "Are There Others?"[74] The note dealt with the *Narrative of the Life of James Allen*, with aliases, the best known of which was George Walton. While waiting for the gallows, Walton, a Jamaican mulatto with an unenviable reputation as a highwayman, gave a signed statement to the warden of the Massachusetts State Prison, and this document was published in 1837 by Harrington and Company of Boston as a slender thirty-page octavo. Shortly after Walton's execution, his tanned hide was delivered to Peter Low, an English binder who had established himself in the Old Corner Book Store. Low matched up the gruesome hide with the lurid contents of the owner's statement, and today this volume, with an inscription reading "Hic Liber Waltonis Cute Compactus Est" rests in the Trustee's Room of the Athenaeum.

Yes, there are others. Indeed, autoanthropodermic binding has its own little cubbyhole in the field of bibilopegy. Back in the days of a happier Berlin of 1913 and 1914 this subject came up in the lively discussions of anthropodermic bindings in the "Kunst and Wissenschaft" column of the *Berliner Tageblatt*; and Bogeng, who could never resist the opportunity to express himself on such occasions, put down a few original speculations on the matter:

> Maybe the ambition of bibliophiles feverishly aroused by the newspaper stories, will turn to a problem never yet solved: the library of books bound in the skin of their own authors. But this library will probably always remain a pious wish, unfulfilled because of the caprice of the object and not of the subje:t.[75]

Essad Bey reflected on the destiny of Walton's mortal remains and stated his personal conviction that even though some might find this practice "repulsive, yes, even immoral," he himself believed that beneath the surface there was a "good spot of piety, of old, coarse romanticism . . ." Those who seek the romantic will probably find no tale of autoanthropodermic bibliopegy quite so fascinating as the story of Percy Fitzgerald in his *Book Fancier* about an unidentified Russian poet who fell from his horse and suffered amputation of a lower extremity which he promptly had flayed and the skin tanned. The resulting leather was used to bind a volume of his own sonnets, which was in turn presented to his lady love.

One of the most famous of all autoanthropodermic bindings is the one which encases a copy of Delille's French translation of the *Georgics*, in the possession of M. Edmond Leroy, an attorney of Valenciennes toward the early part of this century.[76] Leroy's father, Aimé Leroy, while still a young law student, was able to persuade Tissot, Delille's successor in the chair of Latin poetry at the Collège de France, to permit him to go into the room where the cadaver of "the French Virgil" was lying in state. From the corpse of his master he removed two pieces of skin, one from the chest and another from the leg. We have an account of Leroy's exploit in his own words:

> I don't think I was seen by anyone; rich with my little treasure, I left and disappeared at once. Some will perhaps find a little fault with the act I have just confessed. When I got the idea of stealing these fragments, so frail but so precious for me, it overcame me, and I felt myself driven on by my respect for an illustrious dead man . . . and I committed this larceny by way of reverence.[77]

Two particularly interesting examples of autoanthropodermic bindings have not been located in the course of this investigation. The first one is described by Walter Hart Blumenthal[78] as a volume in "an obscure antiquarian shop" near Saint Augustine's Church in Paris, the "most unique (*sic*) book in the whole world." The author of the book was anonymous, but in the center of the front cover was a delicate inlay in the shape of a butterfly which, according to the accompanying explanation, was made of a piece of the author's own skin. The second is a book bound in the skin of Ernst Kauffmann, a young man who was obsessed with the desire of attaining fame in the world of letters but was prevented from attaining this goal by sickness and an early death. In order to win some kind of notoriety, he made a collection of woodcuts by various celebrated German artists, entitling the whole *Zwei hundert berühmte Männer*, and directed that it be bound in his own skin after his death, a wish which was obediently executed. This volume, together with a copy of *Gil Blas*, two volumes of *A Book about Doctors*, and a three-volume work on entomology were all in the collection of anthropodermic bindings owned by a Dr. Mathew Wood of Philadelphia a half a century ago.[79]

The illusiveness of some of the famous examples of human skin bindings and the case with which the facts concerning them are distorted makes the study a difficult one. For example, another Philadelphia physician, John Stockton-Hough, was one of the leading collectors of anthropodermic bindings in America; but the story of his contributions to the science has been seriously mutilated, even to the extent of giving him the wrong Christian name and dating his activities improperly. In the fall of 1940 the late and much lamented *Dolphin* published an article stating that in 1903 a Dr. F. (*sic*) Stockton-Hough was assembling a collection of human skin bindings and was reported to have more than six.[80] It was further stated that he facilitated the binder's work by procuring and tanning the skin himself. The *Dolphin* advised that his collection passed to "the Library of the Philadelphia Hospital, where it may probably still be seen."

The facts of the case are somewhat different. John Stockton-Hough graduated from the University of Pennsylvania Medical School in 1868, and in 1900 he died in Ewingville, near Trenton. The following year his library was sold to the Philadelphia College of Physicians. Two anthropodermic bindings have been identified in the library of the College of Physicians as having formerly belonged to Stockton-Hough, entered in the catalogue of the library as follows:

[Couper, Robert]
    Speculations on the mode and appearances of impregnation in human female; with an examination of the present theories of generation. By a physician.
    149 pp. 8°. Edinburgh, Elliott, 1789.

Contains also 2nd edition of same work.
Volume bound with human skin.

[Drelincurtius, Carolus, 1633–1697]
De conceptione adversaria. Disce, homo, de tenui constructus
pulvere, quae te edidit in luncem conditione Deus. Ed. altera.
[8], 74 pp. por. 24°.
Lugd. Batv., Boutesteyn, 1686.
[Bound with human skin.]
[Portrait inserted.]

With those two models at hand, it is hoped that no library
cataloguer will ever become impatient with the Anglo-
American catalogue rules for failure to give specific instructions on the proper description of anthropodermic bindings.

Both books contain inscriptions by Stockton-Hough stating
that they are bound in human skin. If there are as many as
four more books which were bound by Stockton-Hough, they
cannot be located at present. Dr. W. Brook McDaniel, 2d,
librarian of the College of Physicians, states that some of the
duplicates from the Stockton-Hough collection were sold to
the University of Pennsylvania, while others were sold to various dealers. There is no information available to indicate that
the University of Pennsylvania Library has any of these books
at present. Incidentally, it is of some interest to note that
medical books on both sides of the Atlantic have a special
attraction for anthropodermic binders. Paul Kersten advised
that the University of Göttingen Library owns a Hippocrates
in human skin (pre-Nazi).[81]

The fabulous American book collections have often been
poorly described by Europeans operating with secondary
sources. Two anthropedermic bindings have been discussed so
loosely in Europe that it has been impossible to locate them
or identify the owner. Numerous bibliographical dilettantes
have referred to a *Tristram Shandy* bound in the skin of a
young Chinese woman and a *Sentimental Journey* bound in
the skin of a negress which were supposed to have been in
the collection of a wealthy merchant of Cincinnati, Mr. William G . . . Albert Cim blandly repeats this tale in *Le livre*,[82]

but neither he nor anyone else can give a primary source for the information. Likewise, extensive investigation by the reference department of Cincinnati's efficient Public Library failed to shed more light on the matter. William G . . . is still a bibliographical ghost, if not also the defunct negress and the Chinese girl.

The most frequently misquoted story of a human skin binding in modern times is also the best known and is missing from no respectable study of anthropodermic bibliopegy. It deals with the famous volume owned by Camille Flammarion, French popularizer of astronomical research. As late as 1925 the book was still in the library of the observatory at Juvisy, and it may still be there if some Nazi who never heard of Buchenwald did not liberate it. But between the *American Weekly* and romantically inclined Gallic bibliophiles, the story has been mutilated so that some versions are almost unrecognizable. However, a careful study of the different texts will yield a reasonably accurate narrative.

One tale, and this seems to be the one that has fastened itself on the Gallic mind, has it that a twenty-eight year old countess of foreign (*i.e.*, not French) birth prevailed upon her husband to invite Flammarion to her chateau in the Jura.[83] The young woman was dying of tuberculosis, and she told Flammarion that after her death she was going to have him sent a present which he would be compelled to accept. An anonymous writer in the *Chronique médicale* argues that Flammarion later admitted that on the night of the farewell he had expressed intense admiration for the dazzling white shoulders of the countess. It was not beyond a popularizer like Flammarion to encourage at least a minimum of publicity, and certainly an admission on his part of such a titillating detail improves the story. Nevertheless, the *Chronique médical* is not altogether trustworthy, for it states that the physician who cut away the skin was a Dr. V . . . , whereas other versions attribute the operation to a Dr. Ravaud. On her deathbed the countess is alleged to have told Ravaud that she had secretly loved Flammarion for a long time even though she had never met him. In order for him to remember her, she said, she wanted to have him bind one of his books in her skin. Ravaud identified the countess as a "member of one of the first families of France."

In spite of the fact that Flammarion was alleged to have known the woman and to have admired her shoulders, one is inclined to believe that she was a stranger to him inasmuch as there is an inscription on the volume itself (the Didier octavo edition of Flammarion's *Terres du ciel*) reading "Exécution pieuse d'un voeu anonyme. Reliure en peau humaine (femme) 1882."[84] According to the first story, Flammarion had no way of knowing that the woman desired to have one of his books bound in her skin inasmuch as she did not specify the nature of her proposed posthumous gift. It was also reported in 1927 by the Belgian bibliographer Albert Boukaert that Mrs. Flammarion said that her husband never knew the name of the donor of the leather for binding *Terres du ciel* and that at first he had believed that some medical students were playing a crude trick on him. However, there was a note from Ravaud in the package stating that he (Ravaud) had fulfilled his part of the promise to the dead woman and that he now expected Flammarion to do his part. Mrs. Flammarion still had the note in 1927.[85]

Flammarion reported to Dr. Cabranès, once editor of the *Chronique médicale*, that the binding was executed by Engel. He took the skin, still moist when he received it, to a tanner in the Rue de la Reine-Blanche, and three months were consumed in its preparation. The picture of the binding printed by Blumenthal gives a fairly good idea of this famous piece, but it would be of considerable interest to examine the whole binding in detail to determine whether or not it is hand tooled *au fer froid, style monastique*.

Fortunately, or unfortunately, as the case may be, no other anthropodermic binding has an equally romantic history back of it, although it would surely be interesting to know the full story about the volume in the John G. White Collection at the Cleveland Public Library. It is a Koran purchased from W.

Heffer, the well-known Cambridge dealer in oriental and European books. Heffer advertized that the skin belonged originally to the West Arab leader Bushiri ibn Salim who revolted against his German partners, and he said that the story had been authenticated by a Professor Wilson of Cambridge.

The Newberry Library, like the Cleveland Public, also possesses an anthropodermic binding of oriental provenance. It came to the Newberry Library in 1919 as part of the bequest of Mr. John M. Wing. A note on the front fly leaf reads: "Found in the Palace of the King of Delhi Sept. 21st, 1857, eleven days after the assault. James Wise MD. Bound in human skin." Examination of the pore structure of the leather by a Chicago dermatologist has confirmed the character of the binding. The late Ernest F. Detterer, custodian of the Wing Foundation, states that the binding proper is smooth and thin, almost like parchment, and that it has been dyed a maroon color. The covers have gold stamped corner and center pieces of oriental floral design (accordingly, certainly not of Moslem origin). A letter to Dr. Wise attached to one of the back fly leaves identifies the text of the manuscript as "a narrative of events connected with the Dekkan comprising biographies, deeds, genealogies, etc. of sundry notables by a Nawab Wuzeer of Hyderabad." It was copied by Mir Baki 'Alai, who completed it in the year of the Hegira 1226, that is, 1848, A.D.

In general, American libraries are exceptionally well stocked with anthropodermic bindings, and many of these items are traceable to some of our best known collectors. For example, the Watkinson Library in Hartford, Conn., has an anthropodermic binding from the collection of the late Samuel Putnam Avery. Part of a collection of fine and unusual bindings bequeathed by Mr. Avery to his nieces, the Misses Welcher of West Hartford, it is now on indefinite loan to the Watkinson Library. Rather appropriately, the full title reads *Le traicté de peyne. Poëm allégorique dédié à Monseigneur et à Madame de Lorraynne. Manuscrit inédit du XVIe siècle*

(Paris: Roquette, 1867). Ruth Q. Kerr, librarian of the Watkinson Library, has advised that the binding is light tan in color with gold and dark brown decoration. Evidently it was acquired by Mr. Putnam subsequently to his exhibition at Columbia University in 1903, since it did not find a place in that show, which included several other curious bindings.[86]

Mr. William Easton Louttit, Jr., of Providence, R.I., has three volumes bound in human skin. His copy of Vesalius' *De humani corporis fabrica* (Venice, 1568), is decorated with gold and blind tooling; and the leather label, "humana cute vestitus liber," appeals to the medical historian's sense of the appropriate. Mr. Louttit's copy of the English translation of Adolph Bel's *Mademoiselle Giraud My Wife* (Chicago; Laird and Lee, 1891) is bound in three-quarters leather resembling a dark pigskin; and on the fly leaf is a note reading "Bound in human skin" from the pen of Mr. S. B. Luyster, formerly head of Brentano's rare book department. The book itself was purchased by Mr. Louttit from the Bodley Book Shop in 1936. Most interesting is his copy of *The Dance of Death* (London: George Bell, 1898) by Hans Holbein, with an introductory note by Austin Dobson. The binding is described as "Double gold border, black ⅟₁₆ inch inlay with cross-bones in the corners, black inlay dots and gold arrows, a black inlay circle about one inch in diameter in the center with a gold and black skull inside and crossed gold arrows around . . . Backstrip has black label 'Holbein's Dance of Death' and 1898 in gold with alternate skulls ·and cross-bones between raised hands." The leather is described as "very light in colors."

Anatomist Holbrook Jackson advises that in 1891 an unidentified physician instructed Edwin Zaehnsdorf to bind a copy of Holbein's *Dance of Death* in the skin of a woman tanned by Sweeting of Shaftsbury Avenue.[87] Even though Mr. Louttit's book was not published until 1898, anyone who has tried to unravel the folklore of anthropodermic bindings will recognize the possibility that Jackson's date may be wrong and that Mr. Louttit's volume may actually be the one that was bound by Zaehnsdorf. A phantom copy of the *Dance of*

Death allegedly bound in human skin is said to have been in the Susan Minns Collection sold at auction by the American Art Association in 1922. Mr. Byrne Hackett of the Brick Row Shop believes that he purchased this copy for the late Ganson Goodyear Depew, but it has not been possible thus far to determine precisely what happened to all the books in the Depew library.

A double dose of the bibliographically curious was a miniature volume bound in a strip of leather taken from the back of an enthusiastic collector.[88] This unusual item was in the library of the late James D. Henderson of Boston a decade and a half ago, but it cannot be located since Mr. Henderson's collection has been sold. It is quite probable that it is identical with a book described by Walter Hart Blumenthal as a "tiny putty-gray volume entitled *Little Poems for Little Folks*, published at Philadelphia in 1847, and bound in human skin taken from the arm of a bibliophile . . ." inasmuch as Mrs. Henderson writes that she remembers this as the title of the volume in her husband's library.

A specialist in unusual bindings of all sorts is Captain Maurice Hamonneau, late of the French Foreign Legion and presently of the bookshop of the American Museum of Natural History.[89] One of his most treasured possessions is his copy of Dr. Thomas Bateman's *Cutaneous Diseases* (1818), which is bound in "full morocco", that is, in the skin of a Moroccan negro! For the purposes of record, it might be noted that he bound a copy of *Mein Kampf* in skunk fur,[90] a copy of Champion's *With the Camera in Tigerland* in Bengal tiger fur, and *All Quiet on the Western Front* in cloth from a German uniform.

He bound Mrs. Martin Johnson's works in the skin of an elephant shot by herself and an author's copy of Janet Flanner's *An American in Paris* in delicately etched black kangaroo and calf leather with doublures of silk on which symbolic French figures were painted. Other leathers with which he has operated include the integuments of lions, tigers, zebras (with hair), and Komodo dragons.

The greatest of all American collections, the Library of

Congress, has its example of anthropodermic binding, although the British Museum and the Preussische Staatsbibliothek cannot say the same for themselves. (The staid Bibliothèque Nationale never mentions its example officially, although there are most reliable rumors to the effect that it owns one, *infra*). The Library of Congress' sample is Pablo de Santa Maria's *Scrutinium scriptuarum*.[91] Blumenthal remarks that "The author was a Jew converted to Christianity, and this tract, anti-Semetic in nature, is hidebound in a double sense." The only authority for stating that the volume is bound in human skin is the word of Otto Vollbehr. However, it might be well for Government anatomists to check the binding for vestigal remnants of human hair and correlate their findings with Dr. Vollbehr's dossier. If the leather of the *Scrutinium scriptuarum* at the Library of Congress is actually of human origin, it is in a form that is a convincing imitation of pig skin.

French collectors and men of letters have been quite partial to anthropodermic bindings. The twenty sou edition of Renan's *Life of Jesus* was bound at Nantes about 1906 in human skin and was known to have been in the possession of an unidentified Parisian collector some fifteen years ago, but its present whereabouts is unknown.[92] The skin was allegedly taken from the armpit of an anonymous woman who had died in the Hôtel-Dieu of Nantes shortly before the binding was executed.

Eugène Sue was only living up to a family tradition if he actually had a small quarto of *Les mystères de Paris* published in 1854 bound in the skin of a girl who had loved him. The *Chronique médicale* and Blumenthal have stated that it was in two volumes bound as one and contained a French inscription, which reads in translation: "This binding is from the skin of a woman, and it was made by M. Alberic Boutaille, 1874."[93] De Crauzat reported that a two-volume set of *Les Mystères de Paris* "en pleine peau d'homme" was offered for sale in 1898 for 200 francs by the Libraire Chacornac at the Quai Saint-Michel.

Sue and Delille are not the only figures from French literature whose names are associated with anthropodermic binding. In the *Catalogue de la bibliothèque de M. L. Veydt* issued in Brussels in 1879 we find the following entry:

> Opuscules philosophiques et littéraires, par MM. Suard et Bourlet de Vauxcelles (Paris, Thevet, in-80). *Exemplaire relié en peau humaine,* comme l'affirme une note collée contre la gerbe. Cette note porte les mentions de la provenance, du prix de la reliure et du nom du relieur. Vingt francs, Deromme, 1796. Provenant de la bibliothèque de M. de Musset. Acheté le 15 de sept. 1832.[94]

The *Chronique* médicale's expert logically speculates that the M. Musset is most probably M. de Musset-Pathay, father of the poet, and not the poet himself as some authorities have improperly assumed. Likewise, it is most probable that co-author Suard is "l'honnête et paisible académicien de ce nom."

Bookish men in France are so thoroughly fascinated by the notion of anthropodermic bindings that the Gallic mind has even resorted to pictorial literary symbolism combined with the bibliopegic variety. One lover of unusual bindings, a Dr. Cornil of the Academy of Medicine, senator from L'Allier, and professor of pathological anatomy in the Faculty of Medicine in Paris, managed to find a tattooed skin portraying two knights from the period of Louis XIII in single combat, and he could think of nothing more appropriate than to order his copy of the *Three Musketeers* bound in this hide.

He had another tattooed bit of human integument showing a heart pierced by an arrow, and this was used for binding his copy of *Bubu de Montparnasse*. His binder was René Kieffer, who protected the worthy doctor by calling him Dr. V . . . in his communications to the *Mercure de France* on the matter.[95] Physicians are not the only professional men who must maintain professional secrecy.

According to De Crauzat, Kieffer was the dean of anthropodermic bibliopegists in Paris, and this in a comprehensive sense. For R. Messimy he bound a copy of *Fête foraines* with an inlaid piece of human skin tattooed with the likeness of a wrestler,[96] a copy of *Les trois dames de Kasbah* with inlaid plates of human skin on both covers showing two ladies in states of dress reminiscent of "Sacred and Profane Love,"[97] and copies of *La vie de caserne* and *Le neveu de Rameau* with inlaid tattooed skins portraying musketeers in shako. Messimy was an indefatigable collector of tattooed anthropodermic bindings. Not satisfied with the superb work of Kieffer, he had De Sambleaux-Weckessen bind a *Sahara et Sahel* with an inlaid tattoo of an equestrian knight in armor.[98] Even Firmin-Didot succumbed to this Gallic passion for tattoos when he bound for Edmond Halphen a *Dance of Death* in the skin of a sailor with tattoos portraying exotic love themes side by side with reverent portraits of his superior officers. De Crauzat says that Halphen patriotically presented this volume to the Bibliothèque Nationale, but that institution has made no such fuss over it as it has over the alleged manuscripts on human parchment.[99]

Rivalling the legacy of Camille Flammarion's unidentified admirer was the inheritance of Auguste Reverdin, a surgeon of Geneva in the last century. Reverdin received from the estate of an unidentified friend a sum of money as well as the skin of the legator, acceptance of the latter being a condition of receipt of the former. He cut a small piece of skin from the cadaver's breast and had it tanned at Annecy at an exorbitant price. Having fulfilled the prerequisite of his benefactor for receiving the money, he promptly got rid of the hide by passing it on to Marcellin Pellin, historian of the French Revolution, who used it for binding his copy of the *Almanach des prisions* (1793).[100]

A quick perusal of the columns of the *Intermédiaire* will reveal other anthropodermic volumes in France. In the 1880s a 32mo edition of Horace's *Odes* published by Charpentier was bound in a human hide prepared by M. Portal, archivist of Le Tarn, who still had the book in his possession as late as 1906.[101] J. G. Bord reported that in 1910 a bookstore in the Rue de Seine was offering Lortic's anthropodermic binding of the Marquis de Sade's *Philosophie dans le boudoir*. The dealer alleged that it was in *peau de femme* and that he could identify the *original* owner by name.[102] In the same year the 12ᵐᵒ edition of Legouvé's *Mérite de femmes* was seen on the quais accompanied by a certification from a physician that it was human skin.[103] In an article beginning "Poe et peau . . ." an unidentified contributor to the *Intermédiaire*[104] advised that J. R. Brousse, the poet of the *Maison sur la colline*, had Poes' *Poems* (translated by Mallarmé and illustrated by Manet and Rops) in the skin of Bamboula, a famous negro wrestler of yesteryear.

Paul Combes advised that Dr. Ludovic Bouland, once president of the Société des collectionneurs d'ex-libris et de reliures artistiques, had a gynaecological treatise in the skin of a woman who had expired in the hosptial at Metz or Nancy.[105] The Municipal Library at Mâcon owns L'Abbé Nollet's *Essai sur l'électricité des corps* (1746, in-12) in human skin.[106] Just before the last war the Chéramy sale in Paris offered an octavo edition of Émile Deschancel's *Le bien qu'on a dit des femmes* bound in *peau de femme* (with sworn certification in writing to this effect by three reputable Parisians) and equipped with silken doublures. Offered at the same sale was an 1885 edition of *Poésies d'Anacréon* allegedly bound in the skin of a negress.[107] Soon after the first World War a shop in the Rue Lafayette offered an anthropodermic binding for sale and displayed other articles supposed to have been fabricated from the same skin.[108]

Ever since the first World War the production of anthropodermic bindings has slackened considerably. To the credit of twentieth-century civilization and to the discredit of nineteenth-century romanticism and decadence, the art of binding books in human skin is dying. Whether or not its revival by the Nazis will find imitators under other political regimes is a problem that reaches beyond the speculative powers of a mere bibliophile.

Notes . . .

1. Harry Thurston Peck, ed., *Harper's Dictionary of Classical Literature and Antiquities* (New York: American Book Company, 1896), pp. 1009–1010.
2. i, 210.
3. iv, 64.
4. See also Albert Way, "Some Notes on the Tradition of Flaying Inflicted in Punishment of Sacrilege, the Skin of the Offender Being Affixed to the Church-Doors," *Archaeological Journal,* V (1848), 189–190.
5. J. Ardagh, "Books Bound in Human Skin," *Notes and Queries,* CLIX (Oct. 25, 1930), 303.
6. Walter George Bell, *More About Unknown London* (London: John Lane, 1921), p. 167.
7. *Ibid.,* p. 170. Quekett conducted several other investigations for Way.
8. Hanns Bächtold-Stäubli, "Haut," col. 1583, in his *Handwörterbuch des deutschen Aberglaubens* (Berlin: W. de Gruyter, 1927–), III, 1583–1585.
9. Giovanni Battista Basile, *Il Pentamerone,* i, 10.
10. See also Max Höfler, *Volksmedizin und Aberglaube in Oberbayerns Gegenwart und Vergangenheit* (Munich: E. Stahl, 1888), p. 172.
11. Bächtold-Stäubli, *op. cit.,* cols. 1584–1585.
12. *Oeuvres complètes* (Paris: G. Crès, 1928–), XII, 132–133.
13. Bächtold-Stäubli, *op. cit.,* col. 1585. The yet unprinted article on "Werwolfsgürtel" in the unfinished *Handwörterbuch* is probably being held as classified information at headquarters in Frankfurt a.M.
14. Paul Kersten, "Bucheinbände in Menschenhaut," *Zeitschrift für Bücherfreunde,* new series, II (pt. 2, 1910/11), 263. A slightly garbled version is repeated by Walter Hart Blumenthal, "Books Bound in Human Skin," *The American Book Collector,* II (1932), 119.
15. B. G., "Manuscrits sur peau humaine, *Intermédiaire des chercheurs et curieux,* II (Nov. 25, 1865), 681. Eduard Stucken, *The Great White Gods* (New York: Farrar and Rinehart, 1934), p. 71, speaks of an Aztec girl who was flayed alive by the priests

of her religion. Immediately after this hideous ritual a youth disported himself in the streets clad in her skin. See also p. 563.

16. Alfred Louis Auguste Franklin, *Les anciens bibliothèques de Paris; églises, monastères, collèges, etc.* (Paris: Imprimerie impériale, 1867–1870; three volumes), I, 297, and Albert Cim[ochowski], *Le livre; historique-fabrication-achat-classement-usage- et entretien* (Paris: E. Flammarion, 1905–1908; five volumes), III, 296–297. Cim is the best available general account of anthropodermic bibliopegy. But in spite of his prodigious store of information on the subject, Cim was gullible enough to repeat the impossible tale told him by the binder Georges Mercier (fils) that it was an old tradition to preserve tanned skin of a dead relative for binding a favorite book. See his "Peau humaine tannée," *Intermédiaire des chercheurs et curieux*, LXII (Aug. 20, 1910), 269–271.

17. "Manuscrits sur peau humaine," *Intermédiaire des chercheurs et curieux*, III (Jan. 10, 1866), 19.

18. *The Life of the Icelander Jón Olafsson, Traveller to India, Written by Himself and Completed about 1661 A.D., with a Continuation by Another Hand, up to His Death in 1679* (London: The Hakluyt Society, 1923–1932; two volumes; translated from the Icelandic edition of Sigfús Blondal by Bertha S. Philpotts), II, 160–161.

19. *A Practical Treatise on the Leather Industry* (London: Scott, Greenwood, 1901; translated by Frank T. Addyman), p. 1.

20. Paul Kersten, "Bucheinbände in Menschenleder," *Die Heftlade*, I (1922–1924), 54.

21. "Les reliures en peau humaine." *Chronique médicale*, V (1898), 137. Possibly identical with the skin in M. B. Gautier's Musée anthropologique reported by Ulric (Desaix?), "Les tanneries de peau humaine," *Intermédiare des chercheurs et curieux*, X (Nov. 10, 1877), 652.

22. H. C., "Human Skin Tanned," *Notes and Queries*, third series, IX (Jan. 27, 1866), 89.

23. J. C. L. (of Malta), "Human Skin Tanned," *Notes and Queries*, third series, IX (Apr. 14, 1866), 309.

24. L., "Human Skin Tanned," *Notes and Queries*, third series, IX (Apr. 28, 1866), 359.

25. Holbrook Jackson, *The Anatomy of Bibliomania* (New York: Charles Scribner's Sons, 1932), p. 511, or II, 91, in the two-volume edition.

26. F. A. Carrington, "Human Skin Tanned," *Notes and Queries*, second series, II (Oct. 11, 1856), 299.

27. "Peau humaine tannée" *Intermédiaire des chercheurs et curieux*, LXII (Aug. 30, 1910), 319.
28. *The Anatomy of Melancholy*, edited by Floyd Dell and Paul Jordan-Smith (New York: Farrar and Rinehart, 1927), p. 30.
29. The 1690 edition is owned by the University of Chicago Libraries.
30. *History of Friedrich II of Prussia called Frederick the Great* (London: Chapman and Hall, 1897; eight volumes), III, 65 (book ix, chapter 4).
31. *Tetoniana: anecdotes historiques et religieuses sur les seins et l'allaitement, comprenant l'histoire du décolletage et du corset* (Paris: A. Maloino, 1898), p. 56.
32. "Les tanneries de peau humaine," *Intermédiaire des chercheurs et curieux*, V (Nov. 10, 1869), 640–641. The *Intermédiaire* has numerous references to the Ziska legend which may be traced in the collective indices under the headings "Tanneries de peau humaine," "Reliure on peau humaine," and "Peau humaine tannée."
33. Ernest de Crauzat, *La reliure française de 1900 à 1925* (Paris: René Kieffer, n.d.; two volumes), I, 137; Essad Bey, "Der Einband aus Menschenhaut," *Die literarische Welt*, IV (no. 31, Aug. 3, 1928), 4; and V. Dufour, "Les tanneries de peau humaine," *Intermédiaire des chercheurs et curieux*, VII (Apr. 10, 1874), 179.
34. *Journal des Goncourt* (Paris: Bibliothèque Charpentier, 1851–1884; six volumes [later volumes published by E. Flammarion]), II, 28.
35. G., "Human Skin Tanned," *Notes and Queries*, third series, VIII (Dec. 2, 1865), 463.
36. R. W. Hackwood, "Human Skin Tanned," *Notes and Queries*, third series, X (Oct. 27, 1866).
37. "Human Skin Tanned," *Notes and Queries*, second series, II (Sept. 27, 1856), 252.
38. Dr. Eugene H. Wilson, director of the University of Colorado Libraries, has ferreted out another possible example of human skin dressed like parchment, cited as Item 351 in List 24 of Paul F. Veith, 4117 Dryades Street, New Orleans 15: Gutiérrez (Ioanne), Practicarum quaestionum circa leges regias hispaniae primae partis nouae collectionis regiae liber I. et II . . . cum duplici indice, altero legum regni, altero materiarum. Quarto (Vellum?) (84), 794, (1) pp. Madrid, 1606. $42.50. A manuscript note at end claimed that the binding is the skin of one John Wright. However, the custodians of the Harvard University Law Library, which purchased this volume, have been unable thus

far to identify John Wright or to substantiate this allegation in any other way.

39. L. W., "Human Skin Tanned," *Notes and Queries*, third series, IX (May 19, 1866), 422.

40. Eugène Grécourt, "Tanneries de peau humaine," *Intermédiaire des chercheurs et curieux*, L (Oct. 10, 1904), 540–542.

41. *Dictionaire raisonné universelle d'histoire naturelle* (Lyon: Bruyset frères, 1791; fifteen volumes; fourth revised edition), X, 204 (article on "peau").

42. J. Doran, "Human Leather," *Notes and Queries*, second series, II (Aug. 9, 1856), 119.

43. Egar, "Tanning the Skin of Criminals," *Notes and Queries*, fourth series, XI (Apr. 5, 1873), 292.

44. The literature of tanned human skin and the French Revolution is enormous. In this brief review it is possible only to refer the patient reader to the collective indices of the *Intermédiaire* and such works as Maurice Cousin, *Souvenirs de la Marquise de Créquy de 1710 à 1803* (Paris: Garnier frères, 1855; ten volumes in five; new edition), VIII, 171; Georges Louis Jacques Duval (pseudonym of Georges Labiche), *Souvenirs de la Terreur, 1788–93; précédés d'une introduction historique par C. Nodier* (Paris: Werdet, 1841–1842; eight volumes), IV, 354–355; F. S. Fouillet de Conches, *Causeries d'un curieux* (Paris: H. Plon, 1862–1868; four volumes), II, 171–172; and Joseph-François-Nicolas Dusaulchoy, *Mosaique historique, littéraire et politique* (Paris: Rosa, 1818; two volumes), I, 240.

45. Paul Kersten, "Bucheinbände in Menschenhaut," *loc. cit.*, p. 264, and Joc'h d'Indret, "Religatum de pelle humana," *Intermédiaire des chercheurs et curieux*, XIV (Dec. 10, 1881), 745–747. According to Dr. By, "Religatum de pelle humana," *Intermédiaire des chercheurs et curieux*, XIII (Nov. 10, 1880), 642, Citizen Philippe owned many books with the inscription "Religatum de pelle humana."

46. A. Adcock, *The Footwear Organizer*, June, 1928, p. 86 (soon only in photostat from the British Museum copy).

47. This incorrigible bibliographical gossip solemnly related that he had seen a poster advertising the Meudon tannery and that he had known one Souterre, who had once worn anthropodermic pants of a single piece of leather. See his "Les tanneries de peau humaine," *Intermédiaire des chercheurs et curieux*, VI (Dec. 25, 1873), 460–462.

48. See "Human Bindings," *Book-Lore*, I (1884–1885), 125.

49. Essad-Bey, *op. cit.*, p. 3.

50. See his "Bucheinbände in Menschenleder." *loc. cit.*, p. 54.

51. H. N., "Ein interessanter Prozess wegen eines in Menschenhaut gebundenen Buches," *Zeitschrift für Bücherfreunde*, new series, IV (pt. 2, 1912/13), 473–474.

52. The Italian dealer Luigi Arrigoni also exhibited an anthropodermic binding in Brera in 1879, according to G. A. E. Bogeng, "Kuriosa," *Archiv für Buchbinderei*, IX (1909), 90.

53. According to Kersten's "Bucheinbände in Menschenleder," *loc. cit.*, p. 54, he bound only six books in human skin, four of which went to dealers (Paul Graupe of Berlin, Agnes Straub of Berlin, Reuss and Pollack, and an unidentified dealer in Toplitz), one to Bogeng, and one (DuPrel's *Das Rätsel des Menschen*) to Kersten himself.

54. See also report of investigations by the pathologist Sir Bernard Spilsbury, who accompanied the eight MPs and the two peers at Buchenwald, in *The Daily Mail*, Apr. 28, 1945.

55. UP dispatch by M. S. Handler in *The Washington Times-Herald*, Nov. 17, 1945.

56. No. 159, Mar. 30, 1913.

57. "La peau humaine," *Mercure de France*, CXLII (Sept. 15, 1920), 832.

58. Lyon; Imprimerie veuve Chanoine, 1873; not located in any American library; cited in "Les reliures en peau humaine," *Chronique médicale*, *loc. cit.*, p. 137, note. 1.

59. Told in his "Peregrinations and Prospects," *Colophon*, 1931, pt. 7, p. [4].

60. *Merkwürdige Reisen durch Niedersachsen, Holland und Engelland* (Ulm and Menningen: J. F. Gaum, 1753–1754; three volumes), II, 192.

61. *Op. cit.*, p. 90.

62. J. Charles Cox, "Tanning the Skin of Criminals," *Notes and Queries*, fourth series, XI (Feb. 15, 1873), 139; Walter Salt Brassington, *A History of the Art of Bookbinding, with Some Account of the Books of the Ancients* (New York; Macmillan, 1894), p. 252. Accounts of the trial are in G. Thompson, *New Newgate Calendar* (London; Walker and Company, 1840), pp. 109–172, and George Borrow, ed., *Celebrated Trials and Remarkable Cases of Criminal Jurisprudence* (London: Knight and Lacey, 1825; six volumes), VI, 44.

63. "Einbaende aus Menschenhaut," *Allgemeiner Anzeiger für Buchbindereien*, XLI (Oct. 18, 1929), 1010, and "Reliures en peau humaine," *La Bibliofilia*, IV (1902/03), 333.

64. There is an extensive account by F. S., "Human Leather Tanned," *Notes and Queries*, second series, II (Sept. 27, 1856), 250–251.

65. *The Book Fancier, or the Romance of Book Collecting*, (London: Sampson Low, Marston, Searle, and Rivington, 1886), p. 123.

66. J. P., "Tanning the Skin of Criminals," *Notes and Queries*, fourth series, XI (Apr. 5, 1873), 292.

67. G. A. C., "Human Skin Tanned." *Notes and Queries*, third series, IX (May 19, 1866).

68. G. M. T., "Tanning the Skin of Criminals," *Notes and Queries*, fourth series, XI (Apr. 5, 1873), 292.

69. "Peau humaine tannée," *Intermédiaire des chercheurs et curieux*, LXII (Dec. 20, 1910), p. 941.

70. T. G. S., "Human Skin Tanned," *Notes and Queries*, second series, II (Sept. 27, 1856), 252.

71. Alfred Wallis, "Book Bound in Human Skin," *Notes and Queries*, seventh series, VII (Mar. 30, 1899), 246.

72. "Les reliures en peau humaine," *Chronique médicale, loc. cit.*, p. 135.

73. Brassington, *loc. cit.*

74. *Athenaeum Items: a Library Letter from the Boston Athenaeum*, no. 30 (Feb., 1944), p. 2 (reprinted, with additions in *More Books, the Bulletin of the Boston Public Library*, XIX [May, 1944], 203–204, and in *Notes and Queries*, CLXXVII [Oct. 7, 1944], 166); the follow-up article, "Collector's Item," no. 31 (May, 1944), p. 2; and "Human Binding" (in the column "One for the Book"), *Bookbinding and Book Production*, XL (Sept., 1944), 31, are the most reliable of innumerable accounts of this fabulous item.

75. Bogeng in *Zeitschrift für Bücherfreunde*, new series, V (pt. 1, 1913/14), 79–80 (Beiblatt).

76. Nitran, "Reliures singulières," *Intermédiaire des chercheurs et curieux*, XVI (Dec. 10, 1883), 718.

77. Quoted by Cim, *Le Livre*, III, 300.

78. *Op. cit.*, p. 120.

79. Cim, *Le livre*, III, 295–296, 300.

80. "Curl Up On a Good Book," *Dolphin*, no. 4, fall, 1940, pt. 1, p. 92; "Legatura in pelle umana," *La Bibliofilia*, XIV (1912/13), 116; and Gustave Fustier, "Reliures en peau humaine," *Intermédiaire des chercheurs et curieux*, LXV (May 10, 1912), 629. Mr. Elliott H. Morse, reference librarian of the University of Pennsylvania Library, lent material assistance in securing the true facts concerning the career and anthropodermic experiments of Stockton-Hough.

81. "Bucheinbände in Menschenhaut," *loc. cit.*, p. 264.

82. Another fairly detailed version is in "Reliures en peau humaine," *La Bibliofilia, loc. cit.*, p. 333.

83. We need pay little attention to the statement of the *American Weekly* of Sept. 4, 1932, that she was the Countess of Saint Anges, whoever that was, printing her picture to prove it.

84. From the photograph of the binding printed by Blumenthal, *op. cit.*, p. 122, where an extensive and fairly accurate account of the episode may be found.

85. E. Leclerc, "Reliures en peau humaine," *Papyrus*, VIII (1927), 742.

86. *Catalogue raisonée* (New York: Privately printed, [1903?]).

87. *Op. cit.*, p. 513, and Blumenthal, *op. cit.*, p. 122. Villon, *op. cit.*, reports that Zaehnsdorf also bound two Elzevirs in human skin.

88. James D. Henderson ("scrivener of the news-letter of the LXIV mos."), *Miniature Books* (Leipzig: Tondeur und Säuberlich, 1930), p. 29.

89. A partial bibliography of the numerous articles on Captain Hamonneau's bibliopegistic exploits includes the following: "Bizarre Bookbinder Uses Snake Skin, Skunk Skin, Human Skin," *Life*, XIX (Oct. 22, 1945), p. 148; "Bookbinder Uses Strange Materials," *Popular Science*, CXXXVI (May, 1940), 136; Donald Richmond Barton, "The Book and the Beast," *Natural History*, XLIV (Sept., 1939), 119–122; "No. 1 Cover Man," *Red Book*, LXXXIV (Nov., 1944), 35; Florence von Wien, "Bookbinder; a 60-Second Close-Up," *This Week* (included as Sunday magazine section of many newspapers, *e.g.*, New York *Herald-Tribune*, July 22, 1945), p. 2; and my note in the *Saturday Review of Literature*, XXXVII (June 2, 1945), 19.

90. Jacob Blanck observed in his column on "News from the Rare Book Sellers," *Publisher's Weekly*, CXLVII (June 9, 1945), 2313–2314, that the best possible copy of Adolf Hitler's masterpiece would be in an autoanthropodermic binding. The New York binder Whitman Bennett also managed to disgrace a helpless polecat by using it to adorn Der Fuehrer's opus.

91. Strassburg: J. Mentelin, not after 1470; Stillwell p. 172.

92. C. P., "Pour 'la peau'," *Mercure de France*, CXXXIII (June 1, 1919), 575.

93. Ernst Collin, "Bucheinbände in Menschenleder," *Die Kunstauktion*, III (Sept. 22, 1929), 16, reports a sale in which this volume changed hands in 1878.

94. *Catalogue de la bibliothèque de M. L. Veydt* (Brussels: Oliver, 1879), no. 2414.

95. De Crauzat, *op. cit.*, I, 141–142.

96. Illustration facing p. 148, *ibid.*

97. Illustration facing p. 144, *ibid.*

98. Illustration facing p. 140, *ibid.*
99. *Ibid.*, p. 137. F. Bargallo, "Reliures en peau humaine," *Intermédiaire des chercheurs et curieux*, LXVI (Oct. 30, 1912), 568–569, reports a respectable American matron in Paris who paid large sums for tattoos from the skins of living persons with inscriptions running along the line of "Adèle est leur bien aimée." Dr. By, *op. cit.*, admitted ownership of a bit of skin from the arm of a girl learning the legend "J'aime pour la vie Léon Camuzat."

100. "Reliures en peau humaine," *Intermédiaire des chercheurs et curieux*, LXVI (July 30, 1912), 125–126.

101. A., "Reliures en peau humaine," *Intermédiaire des chercheurs et curieux*, LIII (Feb. 20, 1906), 269–270.

102. "Peau humaine tannée," *Intermédiaire des chercheurs et curieux*, LXII (July 20, 1910), 96–97.

103. Nisiar, "Peau humaine tannée," *Intermédiaire des chercheurs et curieux*, LXII (Aug. 30, 1910), 319–320, and De Crauzat, *op. cit.*, I, 147–148.

104. "Peau humaine tannée," *Intermédiaire des chercheurs et curieux*, LXII (Oct. 20, 1910), 602.

105. "Peau humaine tannée," *Intermédiaire des chercheurs et curieux*, LXII (Oct. 30, 1910), 661–662.

106. "Peau humaine tannée," *Intermédiaire des chercheurs et curieux*, LXII, (Nov. 20, 1910), 771.

107. "Reliures en peau humaine," *Intermédiaire des chercheurs et curieux*, LXVII (June 30, 1913), 859, and De Crauzat, *op. cit.*, I, 148.

108. "Reliures en peau humaine," *Intermédiaire des chercheurs et curieux*, LXXXI (Jan. 30, 1920), 81.